SILVER TRADING 101
SMART STRATEGIES FOR SILVER TRADING BEGINNERS

Usiere Uko

Copyright © 2024 Usiere Uko

All Rrghts reserved.

No part of this publication may be reproduced, distributed, or transmitted in any form or by any means, including photocopying, recording, or other electronic or mechanical methods, without the prior written permission of the publisher, except in the case of brief quotations embodied in critical reviews and certain other noncommercial uses permitted by copyright law.
This publication is designed to provide accurate and authoritative information in regard to the subject matter covered. It is sold with the understanding that the publisher is not engaged in rendering legal, accounting, or other professional services. If legal advice or other expert assistance is required, the services of a competent professional should be sought.
The author and publisher shall not be liable for any loss of profit or any other commercial damages, including but not limited to special, incidental, consequential, or other damages.

ISBN-13: 979-8-329-16627-9

FIRST EDITION

CONTENTS

Title Page
Copyright
INTRODUCTION
PART 1: INTRODUCTION TO SILVER TRADING   1
Chapter 1: The History and Importance of Silver   2
Chapter 2: Why Trade Silver?   5
Chapter 3: Overview of the Silver Market   9
PART 2: UNDERSTANDING THE BASICS   18
Chapter 4: Key Terms and Concepts in Silver Trading   19
Chapter 5: How Silver Trading Works   23
Chapter 6: Market Participants in Silver Trading   27
PART 3: GETTING STARTED WITH SILVER TRADING   31
Chapter 7: Choosing a Forex Trading Platform   32
Chapter 8: Setting Up Your Trading Account   37
Chapter 9: Funding Your Account and Managing Capital   41
PART 4: ANALYZING THE SILVER MARKET   46
Chapter 10: Fundamental Analysis   47
Chapter 11: Technical Analysis   54
Chapter 12: Sentiment Analysis   63
PART 5: TYPES OF TRADING STRATEGIES   70
Chapter 13: Day Trading   71

Chapter 14: Swing Trading	74
Chapter 15. Position Trading	77
Chapter 16: Long-Term Investing	81
Chapter 17: Investing in Physical Silver	85
PART 6: DEVELOPING A TRADING STRATEGY	90
Chapter 18: Choosing Your Trading Strategy	91
Chapter 19: Risk Management	101
Chapter 20: Creating a Trading Plan	109
PART 7: EXECUTING TRADES	117
Chapter 21: Placing Buy and Sell Orders	118
Chapter 22: Timing Your Trades	123
PART 8: TOOLS AND RESOURCES FOR SILVER TRADERS	129
Chapter 23: Trading Platforms and Software	130
Chapter 24: Useful Websites and News Sources	133
Chapter 25: Algorithmic and Automated Trading	136
PART 9: MANAGING YOUR EMOTIONS	139
Chapter 26: Dealing with Trading Stress and Emotions	140
Chapter 23: Common Trading Mistakes and How to Avoid Them	143
PART 10: STAYING UPDATED AND CONTINUING EDUCATION	147
Chapter 28: Keeping Up with Market News and Trends	148
Chapter 29: Joining Trading Communities and Forums	151
Chapter 30: Continuous Learning and Skill Development	154
PART 11: CONCLUSION AND NEXT STEPS	157
Chapter 31: Reviewing What You've Learned	158
Chapter 32: Setting Future Trading Goals	161
Chapter 33: Resources for Further Study	164
APPENDICES	167

Glossary of Terms	169
Frequently Asked Questions	175
About The Author	179
Books In This Series	181
Books By This Author	183

INTRODUCTION
SMART STRATEGIES FOR SILVER TRADING BEGINNERS

Welcome to Silver Trading 101: Smart Strategies for Silver Trading Beginners. In an era where financial markets are increasingly interconnected and dynamic, silver trading presents a unique opportunity for investors and traders to diversify their portfolios, hedge against inflation, and capitalize on market volatility.

This book is designed to serve as a comprehensive guide for those new to the world of silver trading, offering the foundational knowledge and practical strategies needed to navigate this exciting market.

THE APPEAL OF SILVER TRADING

Silver, often referred to as "poor man's gold," has been a valuable commodity for centuries, treasured not only for its monetary value but also for its industrial applications.

Unlike many other financial instruments, silver combines the qualities of a precious metal with significant industrial utility, making it a versatile asset in any investment portfolio. Whether you are looking to invest in physical silver, trade silver futures, or explore silver-based ETFs and CFDs, understanding the intricacies of this market can open up a wealth of opportunities.

WHY THIS BOOK?

Silver Trading 101 is crafted with beginners in mind. We recognize that stepping into the world of trading can be daunting, especially with the myriad of terms, tools, and strategies one must master. This book aims to demystify silver trading, breaking down complex concepts into easily understandable segments. Whether you are a novice investor or someone with some trading experience looking to specialize in silver, this book provides the essential knowledge and tools to help you succeed.

WHAT YOU WILL LEARN

This book is structured to guide you through every aspect of silver trading:

The Basics: We start with the history and importance of silver, exploring its role in both ancient and modern economies.

Market Dynamics: Gain a thorough understanding of the silver market, including key players, supply and demand factors, and the economic indicators that influence silver prices.

Trading Platforms: Learn how to choose the right forex trading platform, set up your trading account, and manage your capital effectively.

Analytical Techniques: Master fundamental, technical, and sentiment analysis to make informed trading decisions.

Trading Strategies: Discover various trading strategies, from day trading to long-term investing, and learn how to create a robust trading plan.

Risk Management: Understand the importance of risk management, including how to set stop-loss and take-profit orders to protect your investments.

Practical Tips: Get practical advice on placing buy and sell orders, understanding different order types, and timing your trades for maximum profitability.

Advanced Topics: Explore advanced topics such as algorithmic trading, leveraging, margin trading, and hedging strategies.

BUILDING A STRONG FOUNDATION

Successful trading is built on a foundation of continuous learning and disciplined practice. This book encourages you to engage actively with the material, practice trading in demo accounts, and gradually build your confidence in live trading environments. By the end of this book, you will not only understand the mechanics of silver trading but also develop the mindset and skills necessary to navigate the markets with confidence and resilience.

MOVING FORWARD

As you embark on your silver trading journey, remember that the markets are ever-evolving. Stay curious, stay informed, and continuously refine your strategies. The world of silver trading is rich with potential, and with the right knowledge and tools, you can turn opportunities into success.

Welcome to **Silver Trading 101: Smart Strategies for Silver Trading Beginners**. Let's begin this exciting journey together.

PART 1: INTRODUCTION TO SILVER TRADING

CHAPTER 1: THE HISTORY AND IMPORTANCE OF SILVER

Silver has played a crucial role in human history for thousands of years. Its allure dates back to ancient civilizations, where it was not only valued for its beauty but also for its practical applications in trade and industry.

From ancient Egypt to the Roman Empire, silver was used to create coins, jewelry, and various artifacts, symbolizing wealth and power.

Ancient Civilizations: In Mesopotamia, silver was used as a form of currency as early as 3000 BC. The Egyptians mined silver to create intricate jewelry and religious artifacts, associating the metal with the moon due to its bright, reflective qualities.

The Roman Empire: Silver was integral to the Roman economy. The Romans mined silver extensively, producing coins that facilitated trade across their vast empire. The durability and relative scarcity of silver made it an ideal medium of exchange.

The Spanish Empire: During the Age of Exploration, the discovery of vast silver deposits in the Americas, particularly in regions such as Potosí (modern-day Bolivia), significantly boosted the Spanish economy. Silver from the New World flooded into Europe, transforming global trade and finance.

SILVER IN MODERN TIMES

In modern history, silver has maintained its importance in various industries and financial systems.

Monetary Use: Silver continued to be used in coinage well into the 20th century. Many countries, including the United States, minted silver coins until the costs of production outweighed the value of the metal itself.

Industrial Applications: Today, silver's unique properties make it indispensable in numerous industrial applications. It is the best electrical conductor of all metals, making it essential in electronics, solar panels, and batteries. Its antibacterial properties are utilized in medical equipment and water purification systems.

Investment: Silver is a popular investment asset, often seen as a safe haven during economic uncertainty. Investors buy physical silver (bullion, coins) and financial products (ETFs, futures) to diversify their portfolios and hedge against inflation.

WHY TRADE SILVER?

Understanding the historical significance and modern applications of silver provides a strong foundation for appreciating its value and volatility as a trading asset. Here are some key reasons why silver is an attractive commodity for traders:

Market Liquidity: Silver markets are highly liquid, meaning that traders can enter and exit positions with relative ease. This liquidity is due to the high volume of silver traded globally.

Price Volatility: Silver prices can be more volatile than gold, providing opportunities for significant short-term gains. Traders who can effectively analyze and anticipate market movements can capitalize on these price swings.

Diversification: Silver offers an excellent way to diversify an investment portfolio. Its price movements can be influenced by different factors compared to other assets, such as stocks or bonds, reducing overall portfolio risk.

Hedging Against Inflation: Like gold, silver is often used as a hedge against inflation and currency devaluation. During times of economic uncertainty, the demand for silver as a store of value tends to increase.

THE GLOBAL SILVER MARKET

The global silver market is influenced by various factors, including industrial demand, mining supply, and geopolitical events. Here are some critical elements that affect the silver market:

Supply and Demand: The supply of silver comes primarily from mining and recycling. The demand stems from industrial applications, jewelry, silverware, and investment. Fluctuations in supply and demand dynamics can significantly impact silver prices.

Economic Indicators: Economic growth, inflation rates, and currency strength are crucial indicators that affect silver prices. For example, a strong economy may increase industrial demand for silver, driving prices up.

Geopolitical Events: Political stability, trade policies, and international relations can influence silver prices. For instance, trade tensions between major economies can lead to increased investment in silver as a safe haven asset.

Technological Advancements: Innovations in technology can create new uses for silver, increasing its demand. For example, the growing adoption of renewable energy sources, such as solar power, has bolstered the demand for silver in photovoltaic cells.

The history and importance of silver underscore its enduring value and multifaceted applications. As a trader, understanding these aspects provides a solid foundation for navigating the silver market.

CHAPTER 2: WHY TRADE SILVER?

Silver trading has gained popularity among investors and traders for various compelling reasons. This chapter explores the unique attributes of silver, the benefits of trading it, and the factors that make it an attractive asset in financial markets. Understanding these reasons will help you appreciate the opportunities silver trading presents and how it can enhance your investment strategy.

THE UNIQUE ATTRIBUTES OF SILVER

Silver possesses several unique characteristics that distinguish it from other precious metals and commodities:

Industrial and Investment Demand: Silver's dual role as both an industrial metal and a precious metal creates diverse demand sources. It is used extensively in electronics, solar panels, medical devices, and jewelry. Additionally, investors purchase silver for portfolio diversification and as a hedge against economic uncertainties.

Affordability: Compared to gold, silver is more affordable, making it accessible to a broader range of investors. This lower entry cost allows small-scale investors to participate in the precious metals market without significant capital outlay.

Volatility: Silver tends to be more volatile than gold, providing opportunities for traders to capitalize on price fluctuations. This volatility can result in substantial short-term gains for those who can accurately predict market movements.

Liquidity: The silver market is highly liquid, with significant daily trading volumes. This liquidity ensures that traders can easily enter and exit positions, reducing the risk of being unable to sell their holdings when needed.

BENEFITS OF TRADING SILVER

Trading silver offers numerous advantages, making it an appealing choice for both novice and experienced traders:

Diversification: Including silver in your trading portfolio can enhance diversification. Silver's price movements often differ from those of stocks, bonds, and other commodities, providing a hedge against market volatility and reducing overall portfolio risk.

Inflation Hedge: Silver, like gold, is often used as a hedge against inflation. When inflation rates rise, the value of fiat currencies tends to decrease, leading investors to seek refuge in tangible assets like silver. This demand can drive silver prices higher during inflationary periods.

Economic Uncertainty: During times of economic uncertainty or geopolitical instability, investors flock to safe-haven assets like silver. This increased demand can result in significant price appreciation, offering traders lucrative opportunities.

Supply Constraints: Silver mining and production are subject to various constraints, including geopolitical factors, environmental regulations, and production costs. These supply constraints can lead to price spikes when demand outstrips supply.

Technological Advancements: Innovations in technology continuously create new uses for silver. For example, the growing adoption of renewable energy sources, such as solar power, has increased demand for silver in photovoltaic cells. This ongoing demand supports long-term price growth.

FACTORS INFLUENCING SILVER PRICES

Several factors influence silver prices, making it essential for traders to stay informed about market dynamics:

Industrial Demand: The industrial sector accounts for a significant portion of silver consumption. Economic growth and technological advancements drive industrial demand for silver, impacting its price. For instance, increased production of electronics and solar panels can boost silver demand.

Investment Demand: Investor sentiment plays a crucial role in silver price movements. Factors such as economic indicators, monetary policy, and geopolitical events influence investor behavior. Positive sentiment towards silver as a safe-haven asset can drive prices higher.

Supply Dynamics: Silver supply is influenced by mining production, recycling, and geopolitical factors. Disruptions in mining operations or changes in environmental regulations can affect supply, leading to price volatility.

Economic Indicators: Key economic indicators, such as GDP growth, inflation rates, and interest rates, impact silver prices. For example, higher inflation often leads to increased demand for silver as a hedge against currency devaluation.

Currency Strength: Silver is priced in US dollars on international markets. Therefore, fluctuations in the value of the US dollar can affect silver prices. A weaker dollar generally makes silver more affordable for international buyers, increasing demand and driving prices up.

Geopolitical Events: Political stability and international relations can significantly influence silver prices. Events such as trade disputes, wars, and changes in government policies can create uncertainty, prompting investors to seek the safety of silver.

WHY BEGINNERS SHOULD CONSIDER TRADING SILVER

For beginners, silver trading offers several advantages that make it an ideal starting point:

Lower Entry Barriers: Silver's affordability allows beginners to start trading with a relatively small investment. This lower entry barrier reduces financial risk and provides an opportunity to learn and gain experience in the market.

Market Accessibility: Numerous online forex trading platforms and brokers offer easy access to silver trading. Beginners can choose from various financial products, such as silver ETFs, futures, and CFDs, to start their trading journey.

Educational Resources: The silver market is well-documented, with abundant educational resources available for beginners. Books, online courses, webinars, and trading communities provide valuable insights and guidance to help new traders succeed.

Potential for Quick Gains: Silver's volatility presents opportunities for quick gains, which can be appealing to beginners seeking to build their trading confidence and experience.

Trading silver offers numerous benefits, from diversification and hedging against inflation to capitalizing on price volatility. Understanding the unique attributes of silver and the factors that influence its price will help you make informed trading decisions. As you delve deeper into the world of silver trading, you'll discover the strategies and tools needed to navigate this dynamic market successfully.

CHAPTER 3: OVERVIEW OF THE SILVER MARKET

Understanding the silver market is essential for anyone looking to trade this precious metal successfully. This chapter provides a comprehensive overview of the silver market, including its structure, major participants, key exchanges, and factors that influence price movements. By the end of this chapter, you will have a solid understanding of how the silver market operates and how to navigate it effectively.

STRUCTURE OF THE SILVER MARKET

The silver market is a global marketplace where silver is bought, sold, and traded. It consists of several components, each playing a critical role in the functioning of the market:

Physical Market: The physical market involves the buying and selling of physical silver, including bullion bars, coins, and jewelry. This market is essential for industries that require silver for manufacturing and for investors who prefer tangible assets.

Futures Market: The futures market allows traders to buy and sell contracts for the future delivery of silver. Futures contracts are standardized agreements traded on exchanges, specifying the quantity, quality, and delivery date of silver. This market is vital for price discovery and risk management.

Over-the-Counter (OTC) Market: The OTC market involves direct transactions between buyers and sellers without the oversight of an exchange. It includes forward contracts, swaps, and other derivatives. The OTC market offers flexibility but involves higher counterparty risk.

Exchange-Traded Products (ETPs): ETPs, such as exchange-traded funds (ETFs) and exchange-traded notes (ETNs), provide exposure to silver prices without the need to hold physical silver. These products are traded on stock exchanges and offer liquidity and ease of access for investors.

MAJOR PARTICIPANTS IN THE SILVER MARKET

The silver market comprises various participants, each contributing to its liquidity and functionality:

Miners: Silver mining companies extract silver from the earth and supply it to the market. The production levels of miners significantly influence silver prices. Major silver producers include companies like Fresnillo, Pan American Silver, and First Majestic Silver.

Industrial Users: Industries that use silver in manufacturing, such as electronics, solar energy, and medical devices, are significant consumers of silver. Their demand for silver affects market dynamics and pricing.

Investors: Investors include individuals and institutions that buy silver for investment purposes. They seek to profit from price appreciation or to hedge against inflation and economic uncertainty. Investors can buy physical silver, futures contracts, or ETPs.

Speculators: Speculators trade silver to profit from short-term price movements. They use technical analysis, market news, and economic indicators to predict price trends and make trading decisions. Speculators provide liquidity and contribute to price volatility.

Hedgers: Hedgers, such as mining companies and industrial users, use futures and other derivatives to manage price risk. By locking in prices for future transactions, they protect themselves from adverse price movements.

KEY EXCHANGES FOR SILVER TRADING

Several major exchanges facilitate the trading of silver, providing a transparent and regulated environment for market participants:

COMEX: The Commodity Exchange (COMEX), a division of the New York Mercantile Exchange (NYMEX), is one of the most prominent platforms for trading silver futures. COMEX sets the global benchmark for silver prices and offers various futures and options contracts.

London Bullion Market (LBMA): The LBMA is a significant OTC market for silver, known for its price-setting mechanism. The LBMA Silver Price is established through an electronic auction process and serves as a benchmark for silver prices worldwide.

Shanghai Futures Exchange (SHFE): The SHFE is a major exchange for silver trading in China. It offers futures contracts that cater to the substantial demand for silver in the Chinese market.

Tokyo Commodity Exchange (TOCOM): TOCOM is another key exchange for silver trading, particularly in the Asian market. It provides futures and options contracts for silver.

FACTORS INFLUENCING SILVER PRICES

Several factors influence silver prices, making it essential for traders to stay informed about market dynamics. Understanding these factors can help traders anticipate price movements and make informed trading decisions.

Supply and Demand

The basic economic principle of supply and demand plays a crucial role in determining silver prices. Key aspects include:

Mining Production: Changes in the output of silver mines can significantly impact supply. If major silver producers reduce production due to lower ore grades, increased operational costs, or regulatory challenges, the reduced supply can drive prices up.

Recycling Rates: The amount of silver recycled from industrial processes and old jewelry also affects supply. Higher recycling rates can increase the available supply, potentially lowering prices.

Industrial Demand: Silver is used in various industrial applications, including electronics, solar panels, and medical devices. An increase in industrial demand, driven by technological advancements or economic growth, can lead to higher silver prices.

Economic Indicators

Macroeconomic indicators impact silver prices by influencing investor behavior and market sentiment:

GDP Growth: Strong economic growth can boost industrial demand for silver, while a recession may decrease it.

Inflation Rates: High inflation often leads to increased demand for silver as a hedge against currency devaluation. Conversely, low inflation can reduce the attractiveness of silver as an inflation hedge.

Interest Rates: Higher interest rates can strengthen the currency, making silver more expensive for foreign buyers and potentially reducing demand. Lower interest rates have the opposite effect, making silver more attractive as an investment.

Geopolitical Events

Political stability and international relations can influence silver prices through their impact on market confidence and economic stability:

Trade Disputes: Trade wars and tariffs can disrupt supply chains and affect industrial demand for silver. For example, tariffs on electronic goods can decrease the demand for silver used in electronics manufacturing.

Wars and Conflicts: Military conflicts and geopolitical tensions can create uncertainty in the markets, prompting investors to seek safe-haven assets like silver.

Government Policies: Changes in regulations, mining policies, or environmental laws can affect silver production and supply. Additionally, policies promoting renewable energy can increase demand for silver used in solar panels.

Currency Strength

Since silver is priced in US dollars, fluctuations in the value of the dollar have a direct impact on silver prices:

US Dollar Strength: A strong US dollar makes silver more expensive for foreign buyers, potentially reducing demand and lowering prices.

US Dollar Weakness: A weaker US dollar makes silver more affordable for international buyers, increasing demand and driving prices up. This inverse relationship means that currency exchange rates are a critical factor for silver traders to monitor.

Market Sentiment

Investor sentiment and market psychology play significant roles in silver price movements:

News and Speculation: Positive or negative news about the economy, mining companies, or industrial uses of silver can influence market sentiment. For instance, news about increased use of silver in emerging technologies can boost prices.

Market Rumors: Rumors and speculation about future market conditions can lead to short-term volatility. Traders often react to perceived market trends, which can amplify price movements.

Technological Advancements

Innovations in technology can create new uses for silver, driving demand and influencing prices:

Photovoltaic Cells: The increasing adoption of solar panels has significantly bolstered demand for silver, as it is a key component in photovoltaic cells.

Electronics: Advances in electronics and the growing demand for consumer gadgets can increase industrial demand for silver.

Medical Applications: Silver's antibacterial properties make it valuable in medical devices and applications. Innovations in this field can lead to higher demand for silver.

HOW TO MONITOR THE SILVER MARKET

Staying informed about the silver market is crucial for making well-informed trading decisions. Here are several effective ways to monitor the market and stay ahead of the curve:

Financial News

Major News Outlets: Follow leading financial news outlets such as Bloomberg, Reuters, and CNBC. These platforms provide real-time updates on silver prices, market trends, and economic indicators that affect silver.

Industry-Specific News: Websites like Kitco and SilverSeek specialize in precious metals news, offering focused insights and detailed analyses pertinent to silver.

Financial Newspapers: Subscribe to financial newspapers like The Wall Street Journal or Financial Times for comprehensive coverage of global financial markets and their impact on silver prices.

Market Reports

Industry Publications: Read market reports from reputable industry publications such as the Silver Institute's World Silver Survey and CPM Group's Silver Yearbook. These reports provide in-depth analysis of supply, demand, and market trends.

Research Firms: Utilize analysis from research firms like Goldman Sachs, Morgan Stanley, and other financial institutions that regularly publish insights and forecasts about the commodities market.

Broker Reports: Many brokers offer market reports and newsletters that provide valuable information and forecasts on silver trading.

Economic Calendars

Tracking Economic Events: Use economic calendars to track important economic events and data releases, such as GDP growth, inflation rates, and employment figures, which can impact silver prices.

Key Data Releases: Monitor key data releases like the U.S. Federal Reserve's interest rate decisions, non-farm payrolls, and manufacturing data, as these can influence investor sentiment and market movements.

Scheduled Reports: Stay aware of scheduled reports like the Consumer Price Index (CPI) and Producer Price Index (PPI), which provide insights into inflation trends and economic health.

Trading Platforms

Real-Time Quotes: Utilize trading platforms and brokers that provide real-time quotes and price feeds for accurate and timely information.

Charting Tools: Leverage charting tools available on platforms like MetaTrader 4, MetaTrader 5, and TradingView to analyze price movements, identify patterns, and make technical analysis.

Technical Analysis Tools: Use built-in technical analysis tools such as moving averages, RSI, MACD, and Bollinger Bands to forecast price trends and make informed trading decisions.

Alerts and Notifications: Set up alerts and notifications on your trading platform to stay updated on significant price movements or market events that could impact your trades.

Social Media and Forums

Engaging with Communities: Participate in trading communities on social media platforms like Twitter, Reddit, and Facebook. Follow influential traders, analysts, and market experts to gain insights and stay updated on market sentiment.

Trading Forums: Join forums such as Trade2Win and Elite Trader to discuss market trends, share insights, and learn from the experiences of other traders.

Hashtags and Groups: Use relevant hashtags (#SilverTrading, #Commodities) and join specialized groups to filter content specific to silver trading.

Specialized Tools and Apps

Market Monitoring Apps: Download market monitoring apps like Investing.com and Yahoo Finance to access real-time market data, news, and analysis on the go.

Economic Data Apps: Use apps like Econoday and Forex Factory to track economic events and data releases that could influence silver prices.

News Aggregators: Utilize news aggregator apps such as Feedly to compile news from various sources into one streamlined feed, making it easier to stay updated.

Understanding the structure, participants, key exchanges, and influencing factors of the silver market provides a solid foundation for trading this precious metal. By staying informed and monitoring market dynamics, you can make informed trading decisions and capitalize on the opportunities presented by silver trading.

PART 2: UNDERSTANDING THE BASICS

CHAPTER 4: KEY TERMS AND CONCEPTS IN SILVER TRADING

Understanding the essential terms and concepts in silver trading is fundamental for beginners looking to navigate the market effectively. This chapter provides a comprehensive overview of the terminology used in silver trading, along with explanations of key concepts that are crucial for developing a solid foundation in this dynamic market.

BASIC TERMS IN SILVER TRADING

Spot Price: The current market price at which silver can be bought or sold for immediate delivery. It reflects the supply and demand dynamics in the market.

Futures Contract: A standardized agreement to buy or sell a specified amount of silver at a predetermined price on a future date. Futures contracts are traded on exchanges and serve as a tool for price discovery and risk management.

Options Contract: An options contract gives the holder the right, but not the obligation, to buy (call option) or sell (put option) silver at a predetermined price (strike price) within a specified period.

Bid-Ask Spread: The difference between the highest price (ask price) that a buyer is willing to pay and the lowest price (bid price) that a seller is willing to accept for a silver asset.

Leverage: The ability to control a larger position in the market with a smaller amount of capital. It amplifies both potential profits and losses.

Margin: The amount of funds that a trader must deposit with a broker to open and maintain a trading position. It serves as collateral and varies depending on the leverage offered.

Liquidity: The ease with which silver assets can be bought or sold without significantly affecting their market price. Higher liquidity reduces transaction costs and enhances trading efficiency.

TECHNICAL ANALYSIS TERMS

Support and Resistance: Levels at which the price of silver tends to find buying support (support) or selling pressure (resistance). They are key indicators used by traders to identify potential entry and exit points.

Moving Averages: A technical analysis tool that smooths out price data by creating a constantly updated average price. Traders use moving averages to identify trends and reversals in silver prices.

RSI (Relative Strength Index): A momentum oscillator that measures the speed and change of price movements. It ranges from 0 to 100 and is used to identify overbought or oversold conditions in the market.

MACD (Moving Average Convergence Divergence): A trend-following momentum indicator that shows the relationship between two moving averages of a security's price.

Chart Patterns: Patterns formed by the price movements of silver on a chart. Common chart patterns include head and shoulders, double tops/bottoms, triangles, and flags, which traders use to predict future price movements.

FUNDAMENTAL ANALYSIS TERMS

Supply and Demand: The fundamental economic principle that determines silver prices based on the balance between the amount of silver available for sale (supply) and the desire of buyers to purchase it (demand).

Inflation: The rate at which the general level of prices for goods and services is rising, leading to a decrease in the purchasing power of a currency. Silver is often viewed as a hedge against inflation.

Economic Indicators: Data points released by governments and private organizations that provide insights into the health of an economy. Key economic indicators that influence silver prices include GDP growth, inflation rates, and unemployment figures.

Geopolitical Events: Political events, such as elections, wars, trade disputes, and changes in government policies, can impact silver prices by creating uncertainty and affecting investor sentiment.

RISK MANAGEMENT TERMS

Stop-Loss Order: An order placed with a broker to sell silver at a specified price, preventing further losses if the price moves against the trader's position.

Take-Profit Order: An order placed with a broker to automatically close a trading position when the price reaches a specified level of profit.

Risk-Reward Ratio: A ratio used by traders to compare the expected returns of a trade to the amount of risk undertaken. A favorable risk-reward ratio indicates that the potential reward outweighs the risk.

Diversification: Spreading investment capital across different assets and markets to reduce overall risk exposure. Diversification is a fundamental principle of risk management in trading.

TRADING STRATEGIES

Day Trading: A trading strategy where positions in silver are opened and closed within the same trading day to capitalize on short-term price movements.

Swing Trading: A trading strategy that seeks to capture gains in silver prices over a period of days to weeks by holding positions overnight or for several days.

Long-Term Investing: A strategy where investors buy silver with the intention of holding it for an extended period, typically years, to benefit from long-term price appreciation.

Mastering the key terms and concepts in silver trading is essential for developing a solid understanding of how the market operates. We will explore these in greater detail in subsequent chapters.

Whether your interest lies in technical analysis, fundamental analysis, risk management, or trading strategies, familiarizing yourself with these terms will empower you to make informed decisions and navigate the complexities of silver trading effectively.

CHAPTER 5: HOW SILVER TRADING WORKS

Silver trading involves buying and selling silver as a financial asset through various platforms and instruments. This chapter explores the mechanics of silver trading, from understanding market participants to executing trades and managing positions effectively. By the end of this chapter, you will have a clear understanding of how silver trading operates and the steps involved in participating in this dynamic market.

MARKET PARTICIPANTS

Traders: Individuals or institutions who buy and sell silver for speculative purposes, aiming to profit from price movements. Traders include day traders, swing traders, and institutional investors.

Investors: Individuals or institutions who buy silver as a long-term investment, seeking to benefit from price appreciation over time or as a hedge against inflation and economic uncertainty.

Hedgers: Companies involved in silver mining, manufacturing, or other industries that use silver may hedge their exposure to price fluctuations by taking opposite positions in the futures market.

Brokers: Intermediaries who facilitate silver trading by executing trades on behalf of clients. They provide access to trading platforms, market research, and other services.

Exchanges: Platforms where silver futures contracts, options, and other derivatives are traded. Major exchanges include COMEX, the London Metal Exchange (LME), and various regional commodity exchanges.

UNDERSTANDING SILVER CONTRACTS

Spot Contracts: Agreements to buy or sell silver for immediate delivery at the current market price. Spot contracts are settled "on the spot," usually within two business days.

Futures Contracts: Standardized agreements to buy or sell a specified amount of silver at a predetermined price on a future date. Futures contracts allow traders to hedge against price fluctuations or speculate on future price movements.

Options Contracts: Contracts that give the holder the right, but not the obligation, to buy (call option) or sell (put option) silver at a predetermined price (strike price) within a specified period.

STEPS IN SILVER TRADING

Market Analysis: Before initiating a trade, traders analyze market conditions using technical analysis (charts, indicators) and fundamental analysis (economic data, news events) to identify potential opportunities and risks.

Placing Orders: Once a trading decision is made, traders place orders through their brokers. Common order types include:

Market Orders: Orders executed at the current market price.

Limit Orders: Orders to buy or sell silver at a specified price or better.

Stop Orders: Orders to buy or sell silver once the market reaches a specified price level.

Execution and Confirmation: After placing an order, the broker executes the trade on behalf of the trader. Traders receive confirmation of the trade, detailing the price, quantity, and execution time.

Monitoring Positions: Traders monitor their open positions closely, tracking price movements and market conditions. They may adjust their positions based on new information or market developments.

Managing Risk: Risk management is crucial in silver trading. Traders use techniques such as setting stop-loss orders, diversifying their portfolios, and managing position sizes to limit potential losses and protect capital.

TRADING STRATEGIES

Day Trading: Buying and selling silver within the same trading day to capitalize on short-term price fluctuations.

Swing Trading: Holding silver positions for several days to weeks to profit from medium-term price trends.

Long-Term Investing: Buying silver with the intention of holding it for an extended period, often years, to benefit from potential long-term price appreciation.

Spread Trading: Taking opposite positions in related silver contracts (e.g., different delivery months) to profit from price differentials.

TOOLS AND PLATFORMS

Trading Platforms: Online platforms provided by brokers that allow traders to access real-time prices, execute trades, and manage their portfolios.

Technical Analysis Tools: Charts, indicators (e.g., moving averages, RSI), and drawing tools used to analyze historical price data and identify potential trading opportunities.

Research and News Sources: Access to financial news, market analysis, and economic data that provide insights into silver market trends and developments.

Understanding how silver trading works involves grasping the roles of market participants, the mechanics of trading contracts, and the steps involved in executing trades. We will explore these in greater detail in subsequent chapters.

By familiarizing yourself with these fundamentals, you can effectively navigate the silver market and implement trading strategies that align with your investment goals.

CHAPTER 6: MARKET PARTICIPANTS IN SILVER TRADING

Understanding the diverse participants in the silver market is crucial for comprehending market dynamics and how prices are influenced. This chapter explores the various players involved in silver trading, their roles, motivations, and impact on market behavior. By gaining insight into these market participants, you will enhance your ability to navigate and anticipate movements in the silver market effectively.

1. TRADERS

Traders are individuals or institutions who actively buy and sell silver with the primary goal of profiting from price movements.

Types of Traders:

Day Traders: Engage in short-term trading, buying and selling silver within the same trading day to capitalize on intraday price fluctuations.

Swing Traders: Hold silver positions for several days to weeks, aiming to profit from medium-term price trends.

Position Traders: Take long-term positions in silver, often holding for months or even years, based on fundamental analysis and macroeconomic trends.

Motivations: Traders seek to generate profits by accurately predicting future price movements. They rely on technical analysis, market news, and economic indicators to make informed trading decisions.

Impact: Traders contribute to market liquidity and price discovery. Their buying and selling activities based on short-term market sentiment can influence short-term price fluctuations.

2. INVESTORS

Investors purchase silver as a long-term investment, aiming to benefit from potential price appreciation or as a hedge against inflation and economic uncertainty.

Types of Investors:

Individual Investors: Retail investors buy physical silver, silver ETFs, or other investment products to diversify their portfolios and protect against economic risks.

Institutional Investors: Hedge funds, pension funds, and other large institutions allocate funds to silver as part of their diversified investment strategies.

Motivations: Investors view silver as a store of value and a hedge against currency depreciation and inflation. They often take a strategic, long-term approach to investing in silver.

Impact: Long-term investors stabilize the silver market by providing consistent demand. Their actions are influenced by broader economic trends and geopolitical developments, impacting silver prices over extended periods.

3. HEDGERS

Companies involved in silver mining, manufacturing, or other industries that use silver may hedge their price risk by taking opposite positions in the futures market.

Types of Hedgers:

Silver Producers: Mining companies lock in future prices of silver to protect against price volatility and ensure profitability.

Industrial Users: Manufacturers secure future silver supplies at predictable prices to manage production costs and mitigate supply chain risks.

Motivations: Hedgers use futures contracts and options to stabilize their cash flows and protect profit margins from adverse price movements in the silver market.

Impact: Hedgers contribute to market liquidity and price stability by balancing the demand and supply dynamics of silver. Their hedging activities reduce price volatility in the physical and futures markets.

4. BROKERS

Brokers act as intermediaries between traders, investors, and the silver market. They facilitate the execution of trades, provide access to trading platforms, and offer market research and advisory services.

Types of Brokers:

Full-Service Brokers: Provide a wide range of services, including investment advice, research reports, and personalized trading support.

Discount Brokers: Offer basic trading services at lower commission rates, catering primarily to self-directed traders and investors.

Motivations: Brokers earn commissions or fees for executing trades on behalf of clients. They aim to provide efficient execution, market liquidity, and valuable insights to their clients.

Impact: Brokers play a critical role in maintaining market efficiency and ensuring fair and orderly trading. They help bridge the gap between market participants and the exchange, facilitating transparent transactions.

5. Exchanges

Exchanges provide a regulated marketplace where silver futures contracts, options, and other derivatives are bought and sold.

Major Exchanges:

COMEX (New York): Leading exchange for silver futures contracts, setting global benchmarks for silver prices.

London Metal Exchange (LME): OTC market for silver, known for its price-setting mechanisms and global participation.

Shanghai Futures Exchange (SHFE): Key exchange for silver trading in China, reflecting regional demand and supply dynamics.

Motivations: Exchanges facilitate price discovery, transparency, and risk management for market participants. They enforce trading rules, ensure market integrity, and provide clearing and settlement services.

Impact: Exchanges establish standardized contracts, set daily price limits, and regulate trading activities to maintain orderly markets. They serve as crucial hubs for silver trading, attracting participants worldwide.

Market participants in silver trading encompass a diverse range of individuals, institutions, and entities, each playing a vital role in shaping market dynamics and influencing price movements.

By understanding the motivations and impacts of these participants, traders and investors can make informed decisions and navigate the silver market more effectively.

PART 3: GETTING STARTED WITH SILVER TRADING

CHAPTER 7: CHOOSING A FOREX TRADING PLATFORM

Selecting the right forex trading platform is crucial for trading silver effectively and efficiently. This chapter guides beginners through the process of choosing a platform that aligns with their trading goals, preferences, and technical requirements. By understanding the key factors to consider and evaluating different platforms, you can make an informed decision that enhances your trading experience and success in the silver market.

UNDERSTANDING FOREX TRADING PLATFORMS

Forex trading platforms are software applications provided by brokers that allow traders to access financial markets, execute trades, and manage their investment portfolios. These platforms vary in features, usability, and compatibility with trading strategies. Choosing the right platform is essential for executing trades smoothly and accessing essential tools for analysis and decision-making.

KEY FACTORS TO CONSIDER

Regulation and Security:

Ensure the trading platform is regulated by reputable authorities, such as the Financial Conduct Authority (FCA) in the UK or the Securities and Exchange Commission (SEC) in the US.

Look for platforms that offer robust security measures, such as encryption of personal and financial data, to protect against cyber threats.

Trading Instruments:

Verify that the platform supports silver trading, including spot silver, silver futures, options, and other derivatives.

Check if the platform offers access to other financial instruments you may be interested in trading, such as currencies, commodities, and indices.

User Interface and Usability:

Evaluate the platform's user interface (UI) and navigation. It should be intuitive and user-friendly, allowing you to execute trades and access tools without confusion.

Look for customizable features that suit your trading style, such as charting tools, technical indicators, and order types.

Trading Tools and Features:

Assess the availability of analytical tools and research resources. Look for platforms that offer real-time market data, news feeds, economic calendars, and technical analysis tools.

Consider if the platform supports automated trading strategies, such as expert advisors (EAs) or algorithmic trading, if you plan to automate your trading.

Execution Speed and Reliability:

Execution speed is critical in trading. Choose a platform with fast order execution and minimal latency to ensure your trades are executed promptly at the desired price.

Check the platform's uptime and reliability. It should have a robust infrastructure and minimal downtime during trading hours.

Fees and Costs:

Compare trading fees, including spreads (the difference between bid and ask prices), commissions, overnight financing charges (swap rates), and any other applicable fees.

Consider if the platform offers competitive pricing and transparent fee structures that align with your trading volume and frequency.

Customer Support:

Evaluate the quality and responsiveness of customer support services. Look for platforms that offer 24/7 support through multiple channels, such as phone, email, and live chat.

Read reviews and testimonials from other traders to gauge the platform's customer service reputation and reliability in addressing issues promptly.

TYPES OF FOREX TRADING PLATFORMS

Desktop Platforms:

MT4 / MT5 Trading Platform: cmcmarkets.com.

Installed on your computer and offer comprehensive features, advanced charting tools, and customization options. Examples include MetaTrader 4 (MT4) and MetaTrader 5 (MT5).

Web-Based Platforms:

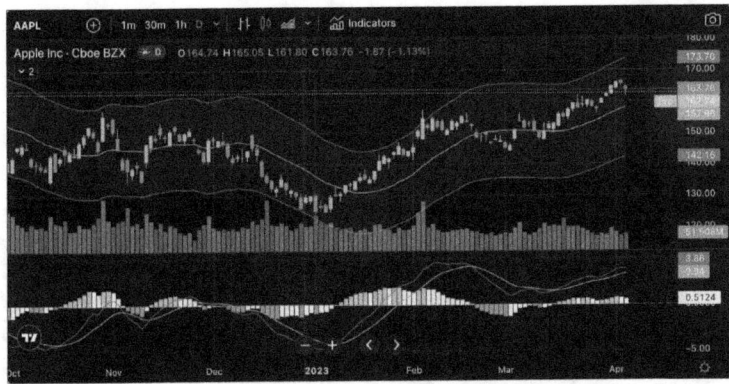

TradingView Desktop Application: tradingview.com

Accessible via web browsers without the need for downloads. They offer flexibility and can be accessed from any device with an internet connection. Examples include TradingView and cTrader.

Mobile Platforms:

Apps designed for smartphones and tablets, allowing traders to monitor markets, execute trades, and manage positions on the go. Examples include MetaTrader mobile apps and proprietary broker apps.

STEPS TO EVALUATE AND CHOOSE A PLATFORM

Research and Compare Platforms: Explore multiple platforms, read reviews, and compare features, fees, and usability.

Demo Accounts: Utilize demo accounts offered by brokers to test different platforms with virtual funds. Evaluate how each platform performs under real market conditions.

Consider Broker Reputation: Choose a broker with a solid reputation for reliability, security, and customer service. The broker's reputation reflects the quality of its trading platform and services.

Scalability and Future Needs: Select a platform that can scale with your trading expertise and future needs. Ensure it supports advanced features and tools as your trading skills grow.

Choosing the right forex trading platform is a critical decision that can significantly impact your trading success in silver and other financial markets. By considering factors such as regulation, trading instruments, usability, tools, fees, and customer support, you can select a platform that meets your trading requirements and enhances your overall trading experience. In the next chapter, we will explore practical steps to set up your trading account, manage your capital, and execute your first trades in the silver market.

CHAPTER 8: SETTING UP YOUR TRADING ACCOUNT

Setting up a trading account is the first practical step towards engaging in silver trading. This chapter provides a detailed guide for beginners on how to establish and configure a trading account effectively. By following these steps, you will be equipped to start trading silver confidently and navigate the complexities of the financial markets with ease.

1. CHOOSING A BROKER

Research and Comparison:

Conduct thorough research on reputable brokers that offer silver trading. Consider factors such as regulation, trading fees, platform features, and customer support.

Compare multiple brokers to find one that aligns with your trading goals, preferences, and level of experience.

Regulation and Security:

Ensure the broker is regulated by a reputable financial authority, such as the Financial Conduct Authority (FCA), Securities and Exchange Commission (SEC), or Australian Securities and Investments Commission (ASIC).

Verify the broker's security measures, such as data encryption and client fund segregation, to protect your personal and financial information.

Trading Instruments:

Confirm that the broker offers a variety of silver trading instruments, including spot silver, silver futures, options, and exchange-traded funds (ETFs).

Evaluate the availability of other financial instruments you may be interested in trading, such as currencies, commodities, and indices.

2. OPENING YOUR TRADING ACCOUNT

Account Registration:

Visit the broker's website and click on the "Open an Account" or "Sign Up" button.

Complete the online registration form with your personal details, including name, address, contact information, and identification documents (e.g., passport, driver's license).

Verification Process:

Upload scanned copies or photos of your identification documents and proof of address (e.g., utility bill, bank statement).

The broker will verify your identity and address to comply with regulatory requirements. Verification typically takes a few business days.

Account Type Selection:

Choose the type of trading account that best suits your needs, such as a standard account, mini account, or demo account for practice.

Consider factors such as minimum deposit requirements, leverage options, and trading conditions offered by different account types.

3. FUNDING YOUR ACCOUNT

Deposit Methods:

Select a deposit method supported by the broker, such as bank wire transfer, credit/debit card, electronic wallets (e.g., PayPal, Skrill), or cryptocurrency (where applicable).

Consider transaction fees, processing times, and currency conversion costs associated with each deposit method.

Minimum Deposit:

Ensure you meet the broker's minimum deposit requirements to fund your trading account. Minimum deposit amounts vary depending on the broker and account type selected.

Currency Selection:

Choose the base currency for your trading account based on your location and preferred trading currency. Common base currencies include USD, EUR, GBP, and others.

4. PLATFORM SETUP AND CONFIGURATION

Download and Installation:

If using a desktop trading platform (e.g., MetaTrader 4, cTrader), download the software from the broker's website and follow the installation instructions.

Alternatively, access web-based platforms directly through your internet browser or install mobile trading apps on your smartphone or tablet.

Login Credentials:

Use the login credentials provided by the broker to access your trading platform or mobile app.

Ensure you securely store and manage your login details to prevent unauthorized access to your trading account.

Platform Customization:

Customize your trading platform settings, such as language preferences, chart layouts, technical indicators, and order types.

Familiarize yourself with the platform's features and navigation to optimize your trading experience.

5. PRACTICE TRADING (OPTIONAL)

Demo Account:

Consider using a demo account provided by the broker to practice trading strategies and familiarize yourself with the platform's functionalities.

Demo accounts allow you to trade with virtual funds in real-market conditions without risking your capital.

Learning Resources:

Utilize educational resources and tutorials offered by the broker to enhance your trading knowledge and skills.

Learn how to analyze market trends, execute trades, and manage risk effectively through online courses, webinars, and trading guides.

Setting up your trading account is a fundamental step towards embarking on your silver trading journey. By carefully selecting a reputable broker, completing the account registration process, funding your account, configuring your trading platform, and optionally practicing with a demo account, you will be well-prepared to start trading silver confidently.

CHAPTER 9: FUNDING YOUR ACCOUNT AND MANAGING CAPITAL

Funding your trading account and effectively managing your capital are essential aspects of successful silver trading. This chapter explores practical strategies and considerations for depositing funds into your account, allocating capital wisely, and implementing risk management techniques to safeguard your investments.

By mastering these fundamentals, you can optimize your trading performance and navigate the complexities of the silver market with confidence.

1. FUNDING YOUR TRADING ACCOUNT

Deposit Methods:

Choose from various deposit methods offered by your broker, such as:

Bank Wire Transfer: Direct transfer of funds from your bank account to your trading account.

Credit/Debit Card: Instant deposit using major credit or debit cards (Visa, Mastercard, etc.).

Electronic Wallets: Fast and convenient transfers via online payment platforms like PayPal, Skrill, Neteller, etc.

Cryptocurrency: Some brokers accept deposits in cryptocurrencies like Bitcoin (BTC), Ethereum (ETH), etc.

Select a method that suits your preferences based on factors such as transaction fees, processing times, and availability.

Minimum Deposit Requirements:

Ensure you meet the broker's minimum deposit requirements for your chosen account type.

Minimum deposit amounts vary depending on the broker and account specifications (e.g., standard account, mini account).

Currency Considerations:

Choose the base currency for your trading account based on your location and trading preferences.

Consider currency conversion costs if your trading account is denominated in a different currency than your local currency.

2. MANAGING YOUR TRADING CAPITAL

Risk Management Principles:

Risk Tolerance: Assess your risk tolerance level and determine how much capital you are willing to risk per trade. For example, if you have a conservative risk tolerance, you might decide to risk no more than 1-2% of your trading capital on any single trade. This means if you have a $10,000 trading account, you would limit your risk to $100-$200 per trade to manage potential losses effectively.

Position Sizing: Calculate position sizes based on your risk tolerance and stop-loss levels to manage potential losses. For example, if your risk tolerance is 2% of your $10,000 trading capital per trade, you would risk $200. If you set a stop-loss at 50 pips for a trade, you can determine your position size by dividing the amount you're willing to risk ($200) by the pip value. If the pip value is $1, your position size would be 200 units of the silver/currency pair.

Diversification: Spread your capital across various silver/currency pairs and trading strategies to reduce overall risk exposure. For example, consider trading pairs like XAG/USD (silver/US dollar), XAG/EUR (silver/euro), and XAG/GBP (silver/British pound) to diversify your trade and mitigate potential losses.

Stop-Loss Orders: Set stop-loss orders to automatically close trades at predetermined price levels to limit potential losses.

Capital Allocation Strategies:

Fixed Fractional Position Sizing: Allocate a set percentage of your trading capital to each trade, adjusting position sizes based on account size and risk. For example, if you have a $10,000 trading account and decide to allocate 2% per trade, you would risk $200 per trade. If your stop-loss is set at 50 pips and the pip value is $2, you can calculate your position size accordingly. This approach ensures consistency in managing risk while allowing for potential growth as your account size changes over time.

Risk-to-Reward Ratio: Evaluate potential returns relative to the amount of capital risked in each trade. Aim for a favorable risk-to-reward ratio, such as 1:3, to optimize profitability. For example, if you risk $100 on a trade, target a potential profit of at least $300. This means if you set your stop-loss at 50 pips, your take-profit should be at 150 pips, ensuring that the potential reward is three times the amount risked.

Pyramiding: Gradually increase position sizes in winning trades while controlling risk, allowing you to maximize profits during favorable market conditions. For example, if you start with 100 units of XAG/USD and the trade is going well, you might add another 50 units as the price continues to move in your favor, rather than investing a large amount upfront.

Monitoring and Adjustments:

Regularly monitor your account balance, open positions, and overall portfolio performance.

Adjust your trading strategies and risk management techniques based on market conditions, profitability, and evolving trading goals.

3. PSYCHOLOGICAL FACTORS

Emotional Discipline:

Maintain emotional discipline and avoid making impulsive trading decisions based on fear or greed.

Stick to your trading plan and predefined risk management rules to mitigate emotional biases.

Continuous Learning:

Continuously educate yourself about market trends, trading strategies, and economic developments.

Stay updated with market news and analysis to make informed trading decisions and adapt to changing market conditions.

4. WITHDRAWAL STRATEGIES

Withdrawal Methods:

Familiarize yourself with the withdrawal methods offered by your broker, such as bank wire transfer, credit/debit card withdrawal, electronic wallets, etc.

Check withdrawal fees, processing times, and minimum withdrawal amounts imposed by the broker.

Profit Withdrawal Plan:

Develop a profit withdrawal plan to systematically withdraw earnings from your trading account while maintaining sufficient capital for trading activities. For example, if you earn $500 in profits from successful trades in a month and decide to withdraw 50%, you would withdraw $250. This approach helps secure gains while ensuring you have capital available for future trading opportunities..

Funding your trading account and managing capital effectively are crucial steps in achieving success in silver trading. By selecting appropriate deposit methods, adhering to risk management principles, allocating capital wisely, and maintaining emotional discipline, you can enhance your trading performance and navigate the silver market with confidence.

PART 4: ANALYZING THE SILVER MARKET

CHAPTER 10: FUNDAMENTAL ANALYSIS

FACTORS AFFECTING SILVER PRICES

Fundamental analysis plays a crucial role in understanding the underlying factors that influence silver prices. This chapter explores the key economic, geopolitical, and industrial factors that impact the supply and demand dynamics of silver. By mastering fundamental analysis, traders can make informed decisions and anticipate price movements in the silver market more effectively.

1. ECONOMIC INDICATORS

Economic indicators play a pivotal role in influencing silver prices and are critical factors that traders and investors monitor closely. Understanding how these indicators impact the silver market is essential for making informed trading decisions.

Inflation and Monetary Policy

Inflation: Silver is widely recognized as a hedge against inflation due to its historical role as a store of value. When inflationary pressures rise, investors often turn to precious metals like silver to preserve the purchasing power of their assets. As a result, higher inflation expectations typically increase demand for silver, driving prices higher.

Interest Rates: Central banks use interest rates and monetary policies, such as quantitative easing (QE), to manage inflation and stimulate economic growth. Changes in interest rates can affect the value of fiat currencies relative to precious metals like silver. For instance, a central bank raising interest rates may strengthen the domestic currency, making silver more expensive for foreign buyers and potentially lowering demand. Conversely, lowering interest rates or implementing QE measures can weaken the currency, making silver more attractive as an alternative investment and boosting demand.

Economic Growth

Industrial Demand: Silver has extensive industrial applications, making it a crucial component in electronics, solar panels, medical devices, and various other industries. Economic growth and industrial activity directly impact the demand for silver. During periods of economic expansion, increased manufacturing and infrastructure development drive up demand for silver in industrial processes. Conversely, economic downturns or stagnation may lead to reduced industrial demand for silver, affecting its price dynamics.

Electronics: Silver's conductivity and durability make it indispensable in electronic devices such as smartphones, computers, and televisions.

Solar Panels: Silver is a key material in photovoltaic cells used for solar energy generation, with demand influenced by global initiatives to adopt renewable energy sources.

Medical Devices: Silver's antimicrobial properties make it valuable in medical applications, including wound dressings, catheters, and surgical instruments.

GDP Growth: Countries experiencing robust GDP growth typically exhibit higher demand for industrial commodities like silver. Economic expansion spurs construction, manufacturing, and infrastructure development, all of which increase the consumption of silver. Therefore, strong GDP growth rates often correlate with higher silver prices as demand rises to meet industrial needs.

2. GEOPOLITICAL FACTORS

Geopolitical factors exert significant influence on silver prices, shaping market sentiment and investor behavior in complex ways.

Geopolitical Stability and Risk

Political Instability: Uncertainty stemming from political instability, conflicts, trade tensions, and other geopolitical events can disrupt global markets. Investors often perceive silver as a safe-haven asset during times of geopolitical turmoil, seeking to protect their wealth from economic and political uncertainties. Consequently, heightened geopolitical risks can increase demand for silver, driving prices higher as investors allocate funds to safer investment options.

Safe-Haven Demand: Silver, alongside gold and other precious metals, is traditionally favored during periods of geopolitical unrest. The metal's tangible value and historical role as a store of wealth attract investors seeking stability and security amidst uncertain geopolitical landscapes. This safe-haven demand can lead to increased buying pressure on silver, influencing its market price.

Currency Movements

US Dollar Strength: Silver prices often demonstrate an inverse relationship with the US dollar. When the dollar strengthens against other major currencies, silver becomes more expensive for holders of those currencies, potentially dampening demand. This relationship occurs because commodities like silver, priced in US dollars globally, require more of the weaker currency to purchase the same amount of silver.

Currency Depreciation: Conversely, depreciation of major currencies relative to the US dollar can enhance silver's attractiveness as an alternative store of value. As fiat currencies lose purchasing power, investors may turn to silver and other precious metals to safeguard their wealth, thereby increasing demand and driving up prices.

3. SUPPLY AND DEMAND DYNAMICS

Understanding the supply and demand dynamics is fundamental to comprehending the factors influencing silver prices in the global market.

Silver Supply

Mining Production: The primary source of silver is mining production, which fluctuates based on various factors such as economic conditions, technological advancements, and regulatory changes. Changes in mining production can significantly impact the overall supply of silver available in the market. For example, a decrease in mining output due to lower ore grades or operational challenges can constrain supply and potentially drive prices higher as demand outpaces availability.

Secondary Supply: In addition to primary mining production, secondary sources of silver supply include recycling and scrap metal recovery. Recycling plays a vital role in replenishing the silver market by reusing silver from discarded electronics, jewelry, and industrial scrap. The availability of secondary supply fluctuates based on economic incentives and technological advancements in recycling processes.

Industrial Demand

Electronics: Silver's exceptional conductivity makes it indispensable in electronic devices such as smartphones, computers, and televisions. It is used in circuit boards, connectors, and touch screens due to its reliability and efficiency in conducting electricity.

Photovoltaics: The increasing global shift towards renewable energy sources, particularly solar energy, has driven substantial demand growth for silver in photovoltaic (PV) cells. Silver's unmatched conductivity and durability enhance the efficiency and longevity of solar panels, making it a critical component in harnessing solar energy.

Medical Applications: Silver's antimicrobial properties make it invaluable in medical devices and healthcare applications. It is used in wound dressings, catheters, surgical instruments, and antibacterial coatings due to its ability to inhibit the growth of bacteria and prevent infections. The healthcare sector's demand for silver continues to grow as advancements in medical technology expand its applications.

4. MARKET SENTIMENT AND INVESTOR DEMAND

Market sentiment and investor demand play pivotal roles in shaping the dynamics of the silver market, influencing price movements and trading activities.

Investor Sentiment

Speculative Trading: Investor sentiment often drives speculative trading in the silver market, leading to short-term price volatility. Traders may react swiftly to news events, economic indicators, or geopolitical developments, resulting in rapid price fluctuations based on market perceptions and expectations.

Investment Demand: Silver attracts investment demand from both institutional investors and retail investors seeking to diversify their portfolios or hedge against economic uncertainties. During periods of market instability or inflation concerns, investors may allocate funds to silver as a store of value, bolstering demand and supporting prices.

Silver ETFs and Investment Products

Exchange-Traded Funds (ETFs): Silver ETFs are investment vehicles that track the price of silver and provide investors with exposure to the metal's price movements without physically owning silver. These ETFs hold physical silver bullion or invest in silver futures contracts, offering liquidity and convenience for investors looking to gain exposure to silver as an asset class.

Futures and Options: Trading in silver futures and options contracts reflects investor sentiment and speculative interest in the market. Futures contracts allow traders to speculate on the future price of silver, while options provide flexibility for hedging strategies or leveraging market opportunities. The trading volume and open interest in futures and options contracts provide insights into market sentiment and the outlook for silver prices.

5. GOVERNMENT POLICIES AND REGULATIONS

Government policies and regulations play a significant role in shaping the operational environment for silver producers and influencing market dynamics.

Taxation and Trade Policies

Tariffs and Import/Export Regulations: Government-imposed tariffs and trade restrictions can affect the flow of silver in global markets. Tariffs on silver imports or exports may increase costs for producers and traders, influencing pricing strategies and market supply. Conversely, trade agreements and reduced tariffs can facilitate smoother international trade flows, enhancing market accessibility and liquidity.

Tax Incentives: Tax policies, including incentives for mining exploration or incentives for renewable energy technologies that use silver, can impact production costs and market competitiveness. Favorable tax regimes may encourage increased silver production or investment in technological innovations, bolstering supply and potentially affecting prices.

Environmental Regulations

Mining and Industrial Sectors: Environmental regulations and sustainability initiatives have a profound impact on silver production and supply chain dynamics. Regulations aimed at reducing carbon emissions, water usage, and waste disposal in mining operations can increase production costs and operational challenges for silver producers. Compliance with environmental standards may require investments in new technologies and processes, affecting supply levels and pricing dynamics.

Sustainability Initiatives: Increasing emphasis on sustainability in the mining and industrial sectors drives innovation and adoption of eco-friendly practices. Silver producers and consumers are increasingly integrating sustainability goals into their operations, influencing supply chain transparency, consumer preferences, and market perceptions.

Fundamental analysis of silver involves evaluating a wide range of economic, geopolitical, supply-demand, and regulatory factors that influence its price movements. By monitoring and analyzing these factors, traders can gain insights into market trends, anticipate price fluctuations, and make informed trading decisions. In the next chapter, we will delve into technical analysis techniques and charting tools used to analyze historical price data and identify potential trading opportunities in the dynamic silver market.

CHAPTER 11: TECHNICAL ANALYSIS
READING CHARTS AND INDICATORS

Technical analysis is an essential tool for silver traders to analyze historical price data, identify trends, and make informed trading decisions based on chart patterns and indicators. This chapter explores the principles of technical analysis, common chart patterns, and key indicators used to assess market trends and potential price movements in the silver market.

1. PRINCIPLES OF TECHNICAL ANALYSIS

Technical analysis is a methodology used by traders to evaluate and forecast future price movements based on historical price data and market psychology. Understanding its principles is essential for interpreting market trends and making informed trading decisions.

Price Action

Historical Price Movements: Technical analysis primarily focuses on studying historical price movements and patterns to identify trends, support and resistance levels, and potential reversals or breakouts. The underlying premise is that market prices reflect all available information and investor sentiment, influencing future price movements.

Market Trends

CHAPTER 11: TECHNICAL ANALYSIS | 55

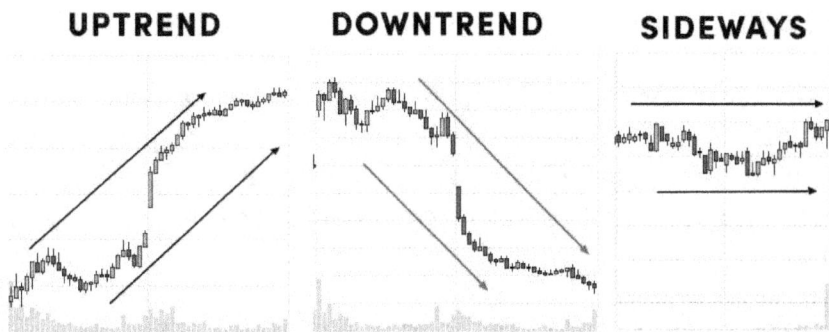

Trend Trading: danielsash.medium.com

Uptrend: An uptrend is characterized by a series of higher highs and higher lows, indicating bullish momentum and increasing buying interest.

Downtrend: A downtrend consists of a series of lower highs and lower lows, signaling bearish momentum and increasing selling pressure.

Sideways (Range-bound): Price movements within a horizontal range without a clear trend direction, often characterized by price consolidations and indecision among traders.

Support and Resistance Levels

Support and resistance: dailyfx.com

Support: Support levels represent price levels where buying interest is sufficiently strong to prevent further decline in price. These levels are identified based on historical price reactions and are viewed as areas where buyers are likely to enter the market.

Resistance: Resistance levels denote price levels where selling pressure is sufficiently strong to prevent further upward movement in price. These levels are determined by historical price peaks and represent zones where sellers are expected to dominate.

Significance: Identifying support and resistance levels is crucial for technical analysts as they provide insights into potential price reversals or breakouts. When price approaches these levels, traders anticipate whether the price will bounce off (reversal) or break through (breakout), informing their trading strategies accordingly.

2. COMMON CHART PATTERNS

Chart patterns are visual representations of price movements on a trading chart that technical analysts use to forecast future price directions and identify potential trading opportunities. Understanding these patterns enhances a trader's ability to interpret market dynamics and make informed decisions.

Reversal Patterns

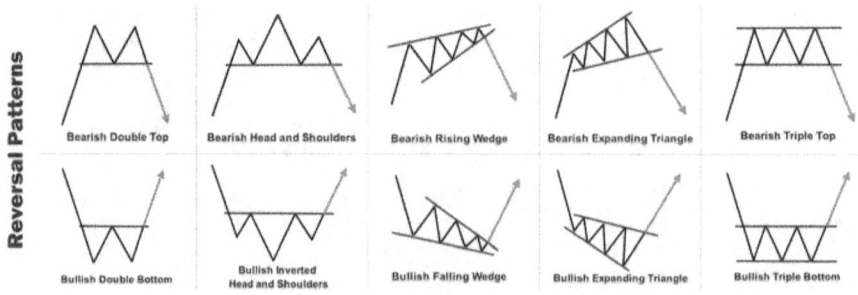

Chart Patterns (Reversal): changelly.com

Head and Shoulders: This pattern typically signals a potential trend reversal from bullish to bearish (or vice versa). It consists of three peaks – the middle peak (head) is higher than the other two (shoulders) which are roughly equal in height. A neckline connects the lowest points of the two shoulders. A breakout below the neckline indicates a bearish reversal, while a breakout above suggests a bullish reversal.

Double Top/Bottom: A double top forms after an uptrend, showing two peaks at approximately the same price level, indicating resistance. Conversely, a double bottom occurs after a downtrend, with two troughs at nearly the same level, suggesting support. Breakouts below the neckline of a double top or above the neckline of a double bottom confirm reversal patterns.

Continuation Patterns

Flags and Pennants: These are short-term continuation patterns that occur within a strong trend. Flags are rectangular-shaped consolidation patterns, where the price moves in a parallel channel after a sharp price rise or fall. Pennants are small symmetrical triangles that form after a sharp move, showing a brief pause before the trend resumes.

Symmetrical Triangle: This pattern forms when two trend lines converge, creating a triangle shape. It indicates indecision in the market as buyers and sellers reach a balance. Traders anticipate a breakout when the price breaches the upper or lower trend line, signaling a continuation of the previous trend.

Breakout Patterns

Ascending Triangle: This pattern forms when the price reaches a horizontal resistance level (upper trend line) and forms higher lows (ascending trend line). It suggests that buying pressure is strengthening, and a breakout above the resistance level could lead to further upward movement.

Descending Triangle: In contrast to the ascending triangle, the descending triangle has a horizontal support level (lower trend line) with lower highs (descending trend line). It indicates that selling pressure is increasing, and a breakout below the support level could lead to further downward movement.

3. KEY TECHNICAL INDICATORS

Technical indicators are essential tools used by traders to analyze price movements, identify trends, and make informed trading decisions. Understanding these indicators enhances a trader's ability to interpret market dynamics and predict future price movements.

Moving Averages

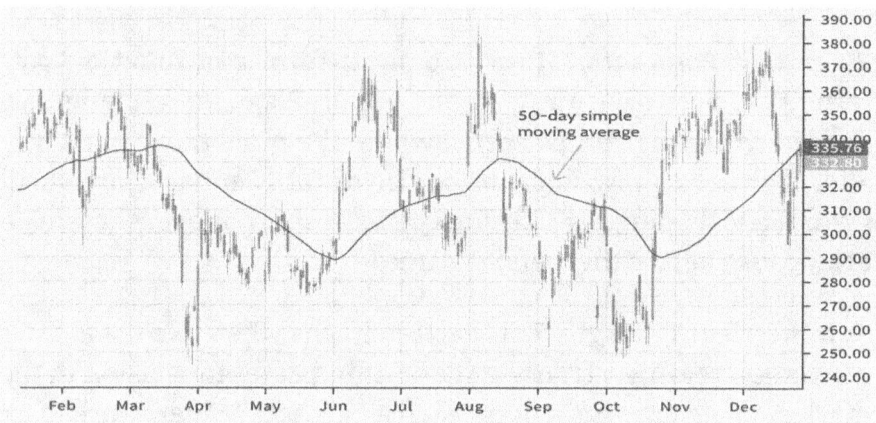

Simple Moving Average (SMA): investopedia.com

Simple Moving Average (SMA): The SMA calculates the average closing prices over a specified period, smoothing out price data to identify trends. Traders use SMAs to gauge the direction of the trend and potential support or resistance levels based on historical price averages.

Exponential Moving Average (EMA): The EMA gives more weight to recent prices, making it more responsive to current price movements compared to the SMA. EMAs are preferred by traders looking for signals based on short-term price trends and crossovers with longer-term EMAs.

Relative Strength Index (RSI)

Simple Moving Average (SMA): investopedia.com

Measurement of Price Momentum: The RSI measures the magnitude of recent price changes to assess whether a security is overbought or oversold. RSI readings above 70 typically indicate that a security is overbought and may be due for a price correction. Conversely, readings below 30 suggest that a security is oversold and may experience a price rebound.

MACD (Moving Average Convergence Divergence)

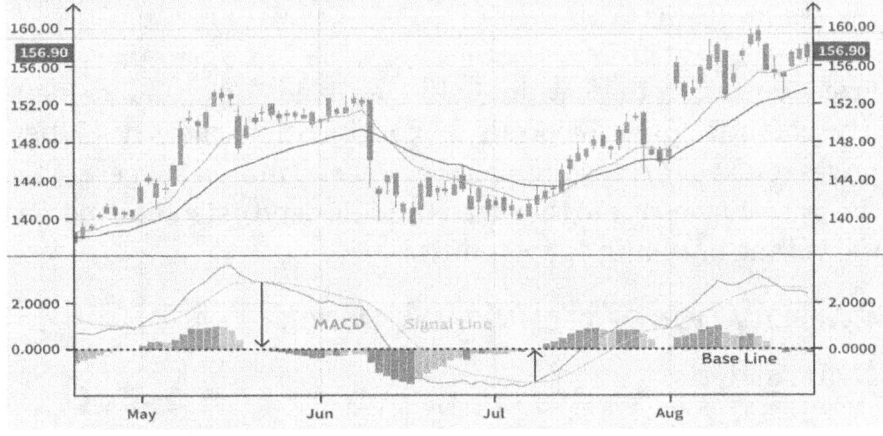

Moving Average Convergence Divergence (MACD): investopedia.com

Trend-Following Indicator: The MACD consists of two main components:

MACD Line: The difference between a short-term EMA and a long-term EMA, indicating momentum and trend direction.

Signal Line: An EMA of the MACD line, providing buy and sell signals based on crossovers with the MACD line.

MACD crossovers (where the MACD line crosses above or below the signal line) and divergences from the signal line are used by traders to confirm trend reversals or continuations.

Bollinger Bands

Volatility Indicator: Bollinger Bands consist of three lines:

Middle Band: A simple moving average (typically over 20 periods), representing the mean or average price.

Upper Band: Positioned above the middle band, indicating higher volatility and representing two standard deviations above the middle band.

Lower Band: Positioned below the middle band, indicating lower volatility and representing two standard deviations below the middle band.

Price Reversion Indication: Bollinger Bands help traders identify potential price reversals or continuation patterns. When prices touch or exceed the upper or lower bands, it suggests that the price may revert to the mean (middle band), signaling potential buying or selling opportunities.

4. APPLICATION OF TECHNICAL ANALYSIS

Chart Analysis

Visualization of Price Movements: Traders use candlestick charts, line charts, or bar charts to visualize price movements over time. Candlestick charts are particularly popular for their ability to display price action, including open, high, low, and close prices, in a visually appealing format that highlights patterns such as bullish/bearish engulfing patterns or doji candles.

Multiple Timeframes Analysis: By examining multiple timeframes (e.g., daily, weekly), traders gain a comprehensive view of price trends and patterns across different horizons. Longer-term charts provide insights into overarching trends, while shorter-term charts help identify entry and exit points within those trends.

Trading Strategies

Trend Following: This strategy involves buying securities that are trending higher and selling those that are trending lower. Traders use trend indicators like moving averages (e.g., SMA, EMA) to confirm the direction of the trend and identify potential entry or exit points.

Breakout Trading: Traders seek to capitalize on price breakouts above resistance levels or below support levels identified through chart patterns such as ascending/descending triangles or rectangle patterns. Breakouts are often accompanied by increased volatility and can signal potential continuation of the trend.

Swing Trading: This strategy involves capturing short- to medium-term price swings within an established trend. Traders identify swing highs and lows using technical indicators and patterns, entering trades at support levels during uptrends or resistance levels during downtrends.

Risk Management

Stop-Loss Orders: Traders set stop-loss orders based on support/resistance levels or volatility indicators to manage risk and protect capital. Stop-loss orders are designed to automatically close a trade if the price moves against the trader beyond a predetermined level, limiting potential losses.

Position Sizing: Traders use position sizing strategies to determine the amount of capital allocated to each trade based on their risk tolerance and account size. Position sizing ensures that trades are proportionate to account equity and risk management parameters, helping traders optimize returns while minimizing potential losses.

Risk-to-Reward Ratios: Evaluating potential returns relative to the amount of capital risked in each trade is crucial for maintaining a favorable risk-to-reward ratio. Traders seek trades where the potential reward outweighs the risk, ensuring that each trade has a clear profit target relative to the level of risk undertaken.

Technical analysis provides traders with valuable insights into market trends, price patterns, and potential price movements in the silver market. By mastering chart analysis, recognizing key indicators, and applying proven trading strategies, traders can enhance their decision-making process and optimize trading outcomes.

CHAPTER 12: SENTIMENT ANALYSIS

UNDERSTANDING MARKET PSYCHOLOGY

Sentiment analysis is a valuable tool for silver traders to gauge market sentiment, investor psychology, and overall market outlook. This chapter explores the fundamentals of sentiment analysis, techniques for assessing market sentiment, and its significance in making informed trading decisions in the dynamic silver market.

1. INTRODUCTION TO SENTIMENT ANALYSIS

Market sentiment analysis is a critical aspect of understanding investor behavior and forecasting potential price movements in financial markets, including commodities like silver. Sentiment analysis provides valuable insights into investor psychology and market dynamics, influencing trading strategies and decision-making processes.

Market Sentiment

Collective Attitude: Market sentiment refers to the overall emotional and psychological outlook of traders and investors towards a specific asset, such as silver. It encompasses perceptions of market conditions, future expectations, and the prevailing mood influencing buying and selling decisions.

Interpreting Investor Emotions: Sentiment analysis seeks to interpret investor emotions, biases, and expectations reflected in market activity. By analyzing factors such as trading volume, price movements, and sentiment indicators, analysts aim to gauge whether sentiment is bullish (optimistic) or bearish (pessimistic) towards silver.

Contrarian View

Opposing Market Sentiment: Contrarian investors employ sentiment analysis to identify situations where market sentiment diverges from fundamental realities or historical trends. They seek opportunities where sentiment extremes (overly bullish or bearish) suggest potential price reversals.

Contrarian Strategies: Contrarian strategies involve taking positions contrary to prevailing market sentiment:

Buying Against Pessimism: When sentiment is excessively bearish (fearful or negative), contrarians may view this as an opportunity to buy silver, anticipating a market bounce-back as sentiment normalizes.

Selling Against Optimism: Conversely, when sentiment is excessively bullish (overly optimistic), contrarians may consider selling silver positions, expecting a potential correction as sentiment cools off.

2. TECHNIQUES FOR ASSESSING MARKET SENTIMENT

News and Media Analysis:

Monitor Financial News: Stay updated with financial news outlets, market reports, and media coverage focusing on silver. News articles highlighting economic indicators, geopolitical events, or industry developments can influence investor perception and market sentiment towards silver as an investment.

Impact of News: Positive news, such as strong economic data or increased industrial demand for silver, may bolster bullish sentiment. Conversely, negative news, such as geopolitical tensions or economic uncertainties, can fuel bearish sentiment among investors.

Social Media and Forums

Track Social Media Discussions: Utilize sentiment analysis tools and platforms like Twitter, StockTwits, Reddit, and Forex Factory to monitor discussions and sentiment surrounding silver. Social media platforms provide insights into retail investor sentiment and potential retail-driven market trends, offering a real-time view of public perception and sentiment shifts.

Retail Investor Influence: Retail investors often express their views and trading activities on social media and forums, influencing short-term market sentiment and contributing to volatility in silver prices.

Commitment of Traders (COT) Report

Weekly Insight into Trader Positions: The COT report, published weekly by regulatory bodies such as the CFTC (Commodity Futures Trading Commission), offers valuable insights into positions held by different categories of traders:

- **Commercial Traders**: Entities hedging against price risks in silver.
- **Speculators**: Investors seeking profits from price movements.
- **Small Traders**: Retail traders participating in the futures market.

Analyzing Position Changes: Changes in trader positioning reflected in the COT report can indicate shifts in market sentiment:

- Increasing speculative positions may suggest bullish sentiment.
- Decreasing commercial hedging activities might signal weakening industrial demand sentiment.

Option and Futures Data

Gauge Institutional Sentiment: Monitor option trading volumes, open interest, and sentiment indicators such as put/call ratios in the options market to gauge institutional sentiment towards silver.

Put/Call Ratios: A high put/call ratio indicates bearish sentiment among institutional traders, suggesting expectations of a decline in silver prices.

Futures Market: Analyze speculative positioning in the futures market to assess sentiment among large traders and institutions:

- Long positions indicate bullish sentiment.
- Short positions reflect bearish sentiment.

3. SENTIMENT INDICATORS AND TOOLS

Sentiment indicators and tools play a vital role in assessing investor sentiment and market dynamics, providing traders with valuable insights into potential price movements in the silver market.

Fear and Greed Index

Composite Sentiment Indicator: The Fear and Greed Index measures market sentiment by analyzing various factors such as volatility levels, market breadth (breadth of stocks advancing versus declining), and put/call ratios in the options market.

Extreme Sentiment Levels: High levels of fear or greed indicated by the index may signal potential market reversals or continuation patterns:

Extreme Fear: Indicates widespread pessimism among investors, potentially signaling buying opportunities as markets may be oversold.

Extreme Greed: Reflects excessive optimism and may indicate overbought conditions, suggesting caution as markets could be due for a correction.

VIX (Volatility Index)

Indicator of Market Volatility: The VIX, often referred to as the "fear gauge," measures expected volatility in the stock market derived from S&P 500 index options. While directly applicable to equities, rising VIX levels generally indicate increased market uncertainty and investor fear:

Impact on Precious Metals: Higher VIX levels can spill over into the silver market, impacting investor sentiment towards risk assets like precious metals.

Hedging and Safe-Haven Demand: Elevated VIX levels may increase demand for safe-haven assets like silver as investors seek to hedge against market volatility and economic uncertainty.

Sentiment Surveys and Indices

Survey-Based Analysis: Sentiment surveys are conducted among various market participants, including institutional investors, analysts, and retail traders, to gauge their outlook on silver prices and market sentiment:

Institutional Investors: Surveys among institutional investors provide insights into consensus expectations and positioning in the silver market.

Retail Traders: Retail sentiment surveys reflect individual investor sentiment and retail-driven trends that can influence short-term market dynamics.

Sentiment Indices: Indices like the Investor's Intelligence Sentiment Index aggregate survey data to quantify bullish and bearish sentiment trends:

- **Bullish Sentiment**: Indicates optimism among market participants, suggesting potential upward momentum in silver prices.
- **Bearish Sentiment**: Reflects pessimism, indicating potential downward pressure on silver prices.

4. PRACTICAL APPLICATIONS IN TRADING

Contrarian Trading Strategies:

Identifying Sentiment Extremes: Contrarian traders seek opportunities where market sentiment diverges significantly from underlying fundamentals or historical trends:

Excessive Bullishness: When sentiment is overwhelmingly positive (bullish), contrarians may consider selling or shorting silver positions, anticipating a potential price correction as optimism reaches unsustainable levels.

Excessive Bearishness: Conversely, when sentiment is excessively negative (bearish), contrarians may view this as a buying opportunity, expecting sentiment to revert and silver prices to rebound.

Anticipating Sentiment Shifts: Contrarian strategies involve taking positions opposite to prevailing market sentiment, assuming sentiment extremes often precede price reversals in the silver market.

Confirmation with Technical Analysis

Validating Trading Signals: Combining sentiment analysis with technical indicators and chart patterns enhances the reliability of trading signals:

Technical Indicators: Use indicators such as moving averages (SMA, EMA), Relative Strength Index (RSI), and MACD (Moving Average Convergence Divergence) to confirm market trends identified through sentiment analysis.

Chart Patterns: Verify sentiment-driven trading opportunities with chart patterns like head and shoulders, double tops/bottoms, and trend lines, aligning technical signals with sentiment indicators.

Enhanced Trade Timing: When sentiment analysis aligns with technical signals, it strengthens trading convictions and improves timing for entering or exiting trades:

- **High Sentiment Alignment**: When sentiment indicators signal extreme bullishness or bearishness and technical analysis confirms trend reversals or continuation patterns, traders have stronger confidence in their trade decisions.

Sentiment analysis offers valuable insights into market psychology, investor sentiment, and potential shifts in silver prices. By understanding and interpreting market sentiment through news analysis, social media monitoring, commitment of traders reports, and sentiment indicators, traders can make informed decisions and capitalize on market opportunities in the silver market. In the final chapter, we will discuss practical tips for risk management, trade execution, and continuous improvement to achieve long-term success in silver trading.

PART 5: TYPES OF TRADING STRATEGIES

CHAPTER 13: DAY TRADING

Day trading is a dynamic and fast-paced approach to trading silver, where positions are opened and closed within the same trading day. This method focuses on capitalizing on short-term price movements and intraday volatility.

Overview

Time Horizon: Day trading involves buying and selling silver positions within a single trading day, ensuring that all trades are closed before the market closes to avoid overnight risk.

Objective: The primary goal of day trading is to profit from short-term price fluctuations and take advantage of intraday volatility in the silver market.

Characteristics

High Frequency: Day traders execute multiple trades throughout the day, relying heavily on technical indicators, price patterns, and intraday market dynamics to make trading decisions.

Quick Decision-Making: Successful day trading requires rapid analysis, timely execution, and decisive action to capitalize on fleeting price movements. Traders must be adept at quickly interpreting market signals and acting on them.

Strategies and Techniques

Scalping: This strategy involves taking advantage of small price movements by making frequent, quick trades throughout the day. Scalpers aim to accumulate incremental profits, which can add up significantly over time. For example, a scalper might buy silver at $25.00 and sell at $25.05 multiple times within an hour.

Intraday Breakouts: Day traders identify breakout patterns and volatility spikes to enter and exit trades within the trading session. For instance, a trader might look for a resistance level at $25.50. If silver breaks above this level, the trader enters a long position, aiming to profit from the ensuing upward momentum.

Considerations

Risk Management: Effective risk management is crucial for day trading. Traders should set strict stop-loss orders to limit potential losses and adhere to position sizing rules to manage intraday volatility. For example, a day trader might risk only 1-2% of their trading capital on any single trade to protect against significant losses.

Market Liquidity: Trading liquid silver instruments with tight spreads is essential to facilitate quick trade execution and minimize slippage. High liquidity ensures that traders can enter and exit positions with minimal impact on the market price. For example, silver futures or major silver ETFs are typically highly liquid and suitable for day trading.

Example of a Day Trade

Preparation: A day trader begins by analyzing the silver market at the start of the trading day. They identify key levels of support and resistance, and monitor technical indicators like the RSI and MACD for potential signals.

Trade Setup: The trader notices a consolidation pattern forming near the $24.80 support level. Based on previous analysis, they expect a potential breakout.

Execution: As soon as the price breaks above $25.00 with increased volume, the trader enters a long position. They set a stop-loss order at $24.75 to limit potential losses.

Monitoring: Throughout the day, the trader monitors the trade, adjusting their strategy based on real-time market conditions. They may use trailing stops to lock in profits as the price moves in their favor.

Closing the Trade: Before the market closes, the trader exits the position at $25.50, securing a profit of $0.50 per ounce. They ensure all positions are closed to avoid overnight risk.

Day trading silver requires a combination of technical analysis, quick decision-making, and robust risk management strategies. By focusing on intraday price movements and employing strategies like scalping and intraday breakouts, day traders can effectively navigate the silver market's volatility and capitalize on short-term trading opportunities. Mastery of these techniques, coupled with disciplined risk management, can lead to consistent profitability in day trading silver.

CHAPTER 14: SWING TRADING

Swing trading is a trading strategy that involves holding positions in silver for several days to weeks. This approach seeks to capitalize on short- to medium-term price swings within an established trend or trading range.

Overview

Time Horizon: Swing trading typically involves holding silver positions for a period ranging from a few days to a few weeks. This timeframe allows traders to capture significant price movements without the need for daily monitoring.

Objective: The primary goal of swing trading is to profit from price fluctuations within an established trend or trading range. Swing traders aim to enter positions at the beginning of a price move and exit before it concludes, capturing the bulk of the market swing.

Characteristics

Technical Analysis: Swing traders rely heavily on technical analysis to make informed trading decisions. They use chart patterns, trendlines, and technical indicators to identify potential entry and exit points based on swing highs and lows.

Patience: Swing trading requires patience and discipline to wait for favorable setups and confirmation of trend reversals or continuation patterns. Unlike day trading, swing traders do not need to make quick decisions but rather focus on the overall trend and market conditions.

Strategies and Techniques

Trend Following: One of the most common swing trading strategies involves following the prevailing trend. Traders enter positions in the direction of the trend, using technical signals and momentum indicators to time their entries. For example, if silver is in an uptrend, a swing trader might buy when the price pulls back to a support level, anticipating a continuation of the upward movement.

Support and Resistance: Swing traders identify key support and resistance levels to anticipate price reversals or breakouts. By placing trades near these levels, traders can take advantage of price bounces or breakouts. For instance, if silver approaches a significant resistance level, a trader might sell, expecting the price to reverse, or buy if a breakout occurs.

Considerations

Risk-Reward Ratio: Evaluating the risk-reward ratio is crucial in swing trading. Traders should ensure that the potential profit from a trade outweighs the potential loss. A typical risk-reward ratio might be 1:2 or 1:3, meaning the expected profit is at least twice or thrice the amount risked. For example, if a trader risks $100 on a trade, they should aim for a potential profit of $200 to $300.

Market Volatility: Monitoring market volatility is essential for swing traders. High volatility can lead to larger price swings and increased risk. Traders should adjust their position sizes based on the volatility levels to manage risk effectively. For instance, during periods of high volatility, a trader might reduce their position size to limit potential losses.

Example of a Swing Trade

Preparation: A swing trader starts by analyzing silver's daily and weekly charts to identify the overall trend and significant support and resistance levels.

Trade Setup: The trader notices that silver has been in an uptrend, and the price has recently pulled back to a support level around $24.00. The RSI indicator shows that silver is approaching oversold conditions, suggesting a potential buying opportunity.

Execution: The trader enters a long position at $24.00, setting a stop-loss order at $23.50 to limit potential losses. The target profit is set at $25.50, where the trader anticipates the next resistance level.

Monitoring: Over the next few days, the trader monitors the trade, watching for any signs of trend reversal or continuation. They may adjust their stop-loss order to lock in profits as the price moves in their favor.

Closing the Trade: When silver reaches the target price of $25.50, the trader exits the position, securing a profit of $1.50 per ounce. The trader ensures that the risk-reward ratio was favorable, with a potential profit significantly outweighing the risk.

Swing trading silver involves holding positions for short to medium durations, aiming to profit from price swings within established trends or ranges. By using technical analysis, swing traders identify key entry and exit points and apply strategies like trend following and support/resistance trading. Effective risk management, including assessing risk-reward ratios and adjusting position sizes based on market volatility, is crucial for successful swing trading. This approach offers a balanced trading style, combining the potential for substantial profits with the flexibility of less frequent trading decisions.

CHAPTER 15. POSITION TRADING

Position trading is a strategy that involves holding silver positions for weeks to months to capitalize on medium- to long-term trends. This approach strikes a balance between short-term trading and long-term investing, focusing on significant price movements driven by fundamental and technical factors.

Overview

Time Horizon: Position trading involves holding positions for an intermediate period, typically ranging from several weeks to a few months. This allows traders to benefit from more substantial price trends without the need for constant market monitoring.

Objective: The primary objective of position trading is to capture significant price movements by aligning with broader market trends. Position traders seek to profit from medium- to long-term price fluctuations while avoiding the noise of short-term volatility.

Characteristics

Trend Identification: Position traders rely heavily on trend analysis to identify and follow significant market movements. They use a combination of fundamental analysis and technical indicators to determine the direction and strength of the trend.

Fundamental Analysis: Evaluating macroeconomic factors, industry trends, and geopolitical events that could impact silver prices is essential. Position traders consider these factors to validate and support their technical analysis.

Technical Analysis: Position traders use chart patterns, moving averages, and other technical indicators to identify entry and exit points. They look for confirmation of trends and avoid frequent trading, focusing on the bigger picture.

Strategies and Techniques

Trend Following: Position traders enter trades in the direction of the prevailing trend. They use technical indicators such as moving averages, trendlines, and momentum oscillators to confirm the trend and determine optimal entry points.

Support and Resistance: Identifying key support and resistance levels helps position traders anticipate potential reversals or breakouts. They place trades near these levels to maximize the risk-to-reward ratio.

Breakout Trading: Position traders look for significant breakouts from established chart patterns or key price levels. They enter positions when the price breaks above resistance or below support, signaling the start of a new trend.

Fundamental Confirmation: Position traders combine their technical analysis with fundamental insights. For example, a trader might hold a position longer if positive economic data supports the continuation of the trend.

Considerations

Risk Management: Effective risk management is crucial for position traders. They set stop-loss orders based on support and resistance levels to protect against significant losses. Position sizing and maintaining a favorable risk-to-reward ratio are also essential.

Patience and Discipline: Position trading requires patience to wait for the right trading setups and discipline to stick to the trading plan. Traders must avoid the temptation to react to short-term market fluctuations.

Market Conditions: Position traders must stay informed about broader market conditions and potential catalysts that could affect silver prices. This includes monitoring economic indicators, geopolitical events, and industry-specific developments.

Example of a Position Trade in Silver

Research and Analysis: A position trader conducts thorough research on silver's market fundamentals and technical indicators. They identify a strong uptrend in silver prices, supported by increasing industrial demand and favorable economic data.

Trade Setup: The trader notices that silver has recently broken above a key resistance level at $25 per ounce, signaling a potential continuation of the uptrend.

Execution: The trader enters a long position at $25 per ounce, setting a stop-loss order at $23 per ounce (below a significant support level) to manage risk. They plan to hold the position for several weeks to months, targeting a price of $30 per ounce based on their analysis.

Monitoring and Adjusting: Over the following weeks, the trader monitors the position, ensuring that the trend remains intact. They may adjust the stop-loss order to lock in profits as the price moves higher.

Exit: If silver reaches the target price of $30 per ounce or shows signs of trend reversal, the trader exits the position, capturing the profit from the medium-term price movement.

Position trading is an effective strategy for capturing medium- to long-term price trends in the silver market. By focusing on trend identification, technical analysis, and fundamental confirmation, position traders can achieve significant returns while minimizing exposure to short-term volatility. Effective risk management, patience, and discipline are crucial to success in position trading, allowing traders to navigate the complexities of the silver market with confidence.

CHAPTER 16: LONG-TERM INVESTING

Long-term investing in silver involves a strategic approach focused on capital preservation, wealth accumulation, and potential appreciation over an extended period. This method requires a deep understanding of fundamental analysis and macroeconomic trends to make informed decisions.

Overview

Time Horizon: Long-term investing in silver typically involves holding positions for several months to years. This extended timeframe allows investors to capitalize on the full potential of market cycles and fundamental trends.

Objective: The primary objectives of long-term investing are to preserve capital, accumulate wealth, and achieve potential appreciation of silver as part of a diversified asset allocation strategy.

Characteristics

Fundamental Analysis: Long-term investors prioritize fundamental analysis to evaluate silver's intrinsic value. Key factors include:

Supply-Demand Dynamics: Assessing mining production rates, recycling activities, and industrial demand helps determine future price movements.

Macroeconomic Factors: Inflation, interest rates, and global economic growth are critical in influencing silver prices. Understanding these factors helps in predicting long-term trends.

Diversification: Silver is included as part of a diversified investment portfolio to hedge against inflation and economic uncertainties. Diversification reduces risk and enhances portfolio stability.

Strategies and Techniques

Buy and Hold: This strategy involves purchasing silver and holding it through market fluctuations. Investors base their decisions on long-term growth prospects, market fundamentals, and historical price performance. The goal is to benefit from the asset's appreciation over time.

Dividend Reinvestment: Investors may choose silver ETFs or mining stocks that offer dividends. Reinvesting these dividends to purchase more shares can compound returns over the long term, enhancing overall growth.

Contrarian Investing: This technique involves buying silver when it is undervalued or during market corrections. Contrarian investors capitalize on the eventual recovery and long-term growth of silver.

Considerations

Market Timing: While the focus is on the long term, aligning entry points with favorable valuation metrics, technical support levels, and broader economic trends can enhance returns. For example, entering the market when silver is trading below its historical average during economic expansion phases can provide a better risk-reward ratio.

Portfolio Allocation: Determining the appropriate allocation of silver within an investment portfolio is crucial. This depends on the investor's risk tolerance and financial objectives. A well-balanced portfolio might include a mix of assets such as stocks, bonds, and precious metals, with silver representing a portion aligned with long-term goals.

Example of a Long-Term Investment in Silver

Research and Analysis: A long-term investor begins by conducting thorough research on silver's market fundamentals. This includes studying global demand trends, mining production forecasts, and macroeconomic indicators such as inflation and interest rates.

Trade Setup: Based on the analysis, the investor identifies a favorable entry point. Suppose silver is currently trading at $22 per ounce, and the investor believes it is undervalued given the increasing industrial demand and potential inflationary pressures.

Execution: The investor buys silver at $22 per ounce, intending to hold it for several years. They allocate a portion of their portfolio to silver, ensuring diversification.

Monitoring and Adjusting: Over the years, the investor periodically reviews market conditions, ensuring the initial investment thesis remains valid. If silver's price appreciates significantly and aligns with their long-term target, they may adjust their holdings or take profits.

Dividend Reinvestment: If the investor has invested in silver mining stocks or ETFs that pay dividends, they reinvest these dividends to purchase more shares, compounding their returns over time.

Long-term investing in silver involves a strategic approach focused on capital preservation, wealth accumulation, and potential appreciation. By employing techniques such as buy and hold, dividend reinvestment, and contrarian investing, long-term investors can effectively manage their portfolios.

Proper market timing and thoughtful portfolio allocation are essential to maximizing returns and achieving long-term financial objectives. This approach allows investors to leverage the unique properties of silver, such as its industrial applications and role as a hedge against economic uncertainty, to build and preserve wealth over time.

CHAPTER 17: INVESTING IN PHYSICAL SILVER

Investing in physical silver can be a valuable addition to a diversified portfolio, providing a tangible asset that serves as a hedge against economic uncertainty and inflation. This chapter will guide you through the various aspects of investing in physical silver, from understanding its benefits to selecting the right types of silver products, ensuring proper storage and security, and making a profit through buying, holding, and selling silver.

UNDERSTANDING THE BENEFITS OF PHYSICAL SILVER

Tangible Asset: Unlike paper assets, physical silver is a tangible asset that you can hold in your hand. This tangibility provides a sense of security, particularly during times of economic turmoil.

Hedge Against Inflation: Silver, like gold, has historically been used as a hedge against inflation. When the purchasing power of fiat currencies declines, the value of silver tends to rise, preserving wealth.

Intrinsic Value: Physical silver holds intrinsic value due to its industrial uses and historical role as a form of money. Its value is not solely dependent on investor sentiment but also on real-world demand.

Diversification: Adding physical silver to your investment portfolio can enhance diversification. It tends to have a low correlation with other asset classes like stocks and bonds, which can help reduce overall portfolio risk.

TYPES OF PHYSICAL SILVER INVESTMENTS

Silver Bullion Coins: Government-minted coins, such as the American Silver Eagle, Canadian Silver Maple Leaf, and Austrian Silver Philharmonic, are popular choices. These coins are typically made of .999 fine silver and are recognized worldwide for their quality and authenticity.

Silver Bullion Bars: Available in various sizes, from one ounce to one kilogram and larger, silver bars are often produced by private mints and refineries. They offer a cost-effective way to accumulate large quantities of silver.

Junk Silver: Coins minted before 1965 in the United States, such as dimes, quarters, and half dollars, contain 90% silver and are referred to as "junk silver." They are often traded based on their silver content rather than numismatic value.

Numismatic Silver Coins: These coins have value beyond their silver content due to their rarity, historical significance, or collector demand. Investing in numismatic coins requires specialized knowledge and can be more speculative.

MAKING A PROFIT WITH PHYSICAL SILVER

Buying Silver: The first step to making a profit is purchasing silver at a favorable price. For example, if the spot price of silver is low due to temporary market conditions, it may be an ideal time to buy.

Holding Silver: Once purchased, holding silver over a period allows you to benefit from long-term price appreciation. For instance, if you bought silver at $15 per ounce and the price rises to $25 per ounce over a few years, your investment's value has significantly increased.

Selling Silver: To realize a profit, you need to sell your silver when market conditions are favorable. Suppose the price of silver peaks at $30 per ounce, selling your holdings at this price would maximize your returns. Monitoring market trends, economic indicators, and geopolitical events can help you decide the best time to sell.

Example: Imagine an investor who buys 100 ounces of silver at $20 per ounce, spending $2,000. After holding the silver for five years, during which industrial demand and inflation drive the price up to $35 per ounce, the investor decides to sell. The silver's value is now $3,500, yielding a profit of $1,500.

PURCHASING PHYSICAL SILVER

Reputable Dealers: Purchase silver from reputable dealers to ensure authenticity and quality. Look for dealers with good reviews, transparent pricing, and clear buyback policies.

Pricing: Silver is typically priced per ounce. Be aware of the spot price of silver and understand that dealers will add a premium to cover manufacturing, distribution, and profit margins. Compare premiums among different dealers to get the best deal.

Authentication: Ensure the authenticity of silver products by purchasing items that come with certificates of authenticity or are produced by well-known mints and refineries. Use tools like scales and calipers to verify weight and dimensions.

STORING PHYSICAL SILVER

Home Storage: If you choose to store silver at home, invest in a high-quality safe that is fireproof and burglar-resistant. Keep the safe in a discreet location and limit the number of people who know about it.

Bank Safe Deposit Boxes: Safe deposit boxes offer secure storage outside your home. However, they may have limitations on insurance coverage, accessibility, and size.

Professional Storage Facilities: Some investors prefer to use professional storage facilities or depositories that specialize in precious metals. These facilities offer high levels of security, insurance, and sometimes even the ability to trade directly from storage.

INSURANCE AND SECURITY

Insurance: Consider insuring your physical silver to protect against theft, loss, or damage. Check if your homeowner's insurance policy covers precious metals or if you need a separate policy.

Security Measures: Implement additional security measures, such as alarm systems, surveillance cameras, and motion detectors, to protect your investment. Always be cautious about discussing your silver holdings publicly.

SELLING PHYSICAL SILVER

Market Conditions: Monitor the silver market and economic indicators to identify favorable selling conditions. Selling during periods of high demand or price spikes can maximize your returns.

Dealer Buyback: Many reputable dealers offer buyback programs. Ensure you understand their buyback terms, including any fees or conditions.

Private Sales: Selling silver privately can sometimes yield higher prices, but it involves more risk. Ensure you take appropriate precautions and verify the buyer's credentials.

Investing in physical silver offers numerous benefits, including its role as a hedge against inflation, a tangible asset, and a means of diversification. By understanding the different types of physical silver, purchasing from reputable dealers, ensuring proper storage and security, and knowing the best practices for buying, holding, and selling, you can effectively integrate physical silver into your investment strategy and maximize your profits. This chapter provides the foundational knowledge you need to confidently navigate the world of physical silver investing.

PART 6: DEVELOPING A TRADING STRATEGY

CHAPTER 18: CHOOSING YOUR TRADING STRATEGY

Choosing the right trading strategy is a critical step in your journey as a silver trader. The right strategy aligns with your financial goals, risk tolerance, and market outlook. In this chapter, we'll guide you on how to select a trading strategy that suits your individual needs, particularly if you're a beginner.

ASSESSING YOUR FINANCIAL GOALS

Choosing the right trading strategy begins with a clear understanding of your financial goals. Different strategies cater to different objectives, and aligning your strategy with your goals will help you trade more effectively. Let's delve into the two main aspects of financial goals: short-term vs. long-term objectives, and income generation vs. wealth preservation.

Short-Term vs. Long-Term Objectives:

Short-Term Goals: If your aim is to generate quick profits, you might prefer strategies that capitalize on short-term price movements. Day trading and swing trading are typical examples of short-term trading strategies.

Long-Term If your goal is to build wealth over time, long-term investing or position trading might be more appropriate. These strategies focus on the bigger picture and are less affected by short-term price fluctuations.

Income Generation vs. Wealth Preservation:

Income Generation:

Frequent Trades: Strategies focusing on frequent trades and leveraging small price changes can provide regular income. These strategies are suitable for traders looking to generate consistent profits on a regular basis.

Scalping: This is a high-frequency trading strategy where traders make multiple trades throughout the day to take advantage of small price movements. For example, a scalper might execute dozens of trades in a single day, each aiming to profit from tiny price changes in the silver market.

Short-Term Trading: Both day trading and swing trading fall under this category. They require active market monitoring and quick execution. For instance, a day trader might enter and exit several trades within a day, aiming for small but consistent gains.

Wealth Preservation:

Less Frequent Trading: Strategies involving less frequent trading and a focus on long-term appreciation are better for preserving and growing wealth over time. These strategies are suitable for investors who are more risk-averse and prefer steady growth.

Buy and Hold: This long-term strategy involves purchasing silver and holding it for an extended period. The goal is to benefit from the overall appreciation of silver's value over time. For example, an investor might buy silver during an economic downturn and hold it for several years until the market recovers and prices increase.

Diversified Portfolio: Incorporating silver into a diversified investment portfolio can also help in wealth preservation. By spreading investments across various asset classes, investors can reduce risk and enhance the stability of their portfolio. For instance, an investor might allocate a portion of their portfolio to silver along with stocks, bonds, and real estate.

BALANCING BOTH OBJECTIVES

Many traders and investors find a balance between short-term and long-term goals, as well as income generation and wealth preservation. This approach can involve:

Hybrid Strategies: Combining elements of short-term trading and long-term investing. For example, an investor might use long-term strategies for their core portfolio while engaging in short-term trades with a smaller portion of their capital.

Adaptive Approach: Adjusting strategies based on changing market conditions and personal financial goals. For instance, during periods of high market volatility, a trader might shift from long-term investing to short-term trading to capitalize on price movements.

By thoroughly assessing your financial goals, you can select a trading strategy that not only aligns with your objectives but also adapts to your evolving needs and market dynamics.

EVALUATING YOUR RISK TOLERANCE

Assessing your risk tolerance is crucial when choosing a trading strategy. It involves understanding your comfort level with risk and aligning it with the inherent risks of different trading approaches. Here's how you can evaluate your risk tolerance:

Understanding Risk

1. High Risk:

Day Trading: Strategies like day trading involve frequent buying and selling of assets within the same trading day. This strategy can lead to significant gains but also exposes traders to high market volatility and rapid price fluctuations.

Example: A day trader might buy silver early in the trading session based on a technical setup, only to sell it later in the day as market sentiment shifts due to unexpected economic news.

Short-Term Strategies: Other short-term strategies, such as scalping or intraday breakout trading, also fall into this category. These strategies require quick decision-making and may result in substantial losses if trades go against expectations.

2. Low Risk:

Long-Term Investing: Strategies focused on long-term investing generally carry lower risk because they aim to capitalize on gradual market movements and fundamental changes over an extended period.

Example: An investor might buy physical silver coins or bars and hold them for several years to benefit from long-term price appreciation and as a hedge against inflation.

Position Trading: This strategy involves holding positions for weeks to months, allowing traders to ride major market trends without being overly exposed to short-term market volatility.

Example: A position trader might accumulate silver during a market downturn, expecting prices to rise over the coming months based on supply-demand dynamics and economic indicators.

Personal Comfort with Risk

1. High Comfort:

Aggressive Strategies: If you are comfortable with taking risks and have the financial capability to withstand potential losses, more aggressive trading strategies might be suitable.

Example: A trader with high risk tolerance might engage in options trading on silver futures contracts, leveraging their capital to potentially amplify returns but with a higher risk of loss.

Active Trading: Strategies that involve active monitoring and frequent trades, such as day trading or speculative trading in silver derivatives, may align with high-risk tolerance investors.

Example: An investor comfortable with risk might trade silver options, where they can profit from price movements without owning the underlying asset, but must manage potential losses carefully.

2. Low Comfort:

Conservative Strategies: If you prefer steady growth and lower risk, consider strategies with longer time horizons and less frequent trading activity.

Example: An investor with low risk tolerance might allocate a portion of their portfolio to physical silver as a long-term investment, focusing on wealth preservation rather than short-term gains.

Diversified Portfolio: Building a diversified investment portfolio that includes silver alongside less volatile assets like bonds and mutual funds can help mitigate risk and stabilize overall returns.

Example: A conservative investor might hold physical silver as part of a diversified portfolio that also includes stocks and bonds, aiming for balanced returns while minimizing exposure to market volatility.

Finding the Right Balance

It's essential to strike a balance between your risk tolerance and the trading strategy you choose. This balance can evolve over time as your financial situation and market conditions change. Regularly reassessing your risk tolerance and adjusting your strategy accordingly can help you achieve your financial goals while managing potential risks effectively.

DETERMINING YOUR TIME COMMITMENT

Choosing the right trading strategy involves evaluating how much time you can dedicate to trading activities. Your availability and lifestyle considerations play crucial roles in determining which approach best suits your circumstances. Here's how to assess your time commitment:

Time Availability

1. Full-Time Commitment:

Day Trading: Day trading requires active monitoring of the markets throughout the trading day, making it suitable for individuals who can dedicate several hours daily to trading activities.

Example: A full-time trader might actively monitor silver price movements using technical analysis tools and execute multiple trades daily based on intraday price fluctuations.

High-Frequency Strategies: Strategies like scalping, which involve quick trades and frequent monitoring, also fall under this category and require a significant time commitment.

2. Part-Time Commitment:

Swing Trading: Swing trading involves holding positions for several days to weeks, allowing traders to capitalize on short- to medium-term price swings. It requires less frequent monitoring compared to day trading.

Example: A part-time trader might analyze silver price charts over the weekend and place trades based on technical indicators and swing trading strategies during evenings or weekends.

Position Trading: This strategy involves holding positions for weeks to months, making it suitable for individuals who can spare a few hours weekly for market analysis and trade management.

Example: A trader with a part-time commitment might accumulate silver positions based on fundamental analysis and hold them for several months to benefit from long-term price trends.

3. Minimal Time Commitment:

Long-Term Investing: Long-term investing in silver requires minimal day-to-day monitoring, focusing on broader economic trends and fundamental analysis.

Example: An investor with limited time might purchase physical silver or invest in silver ETFs, periodically reviewing their investments and making adjustments based on long-term financial goals.

Passive Strategies: Strategies that involve less frequent trading, such as buy-and-hold approaches with periodic rebalancing, are suitable for those with minimal time to dedicate to market activities.

Lifestyle Considerations

1. Alignment with Daily Routine:

Work-Life Balance: Choose a trading strategy that complements your daily routine and personal obligations to avoid undue stress and maintain a healthy work-life balance.

Example: A trader with a demanding job might opt for swing trading or position trading, allowing for flexibility in trading decisions without constant monitoring during work hours.

Flexible Strategies: Consider strategies that allow for adjustments based on lifestyle changes and unforeseen events, ensuring trading activities do not interfere with other priorities.

2. Stress Management:

Emotional Well-Being: Avoid strategies that cause undue stress or anxiety due to constant monitoring or high-frequency trading activities. Opt for strategies that align with your risk tolerance and psychological comfort.

Example: Choosing swing trading over day trading can reduce stress levels by allowing more time for analysis and decision-making, thereby promoting better emotional well-being.

Finding Your Ideal Strategy

Finding the right balance between time commitment, lifestyle considerations, and trading goals is essential for long-term success in the markets. Regularly assess your availability and adjust your trading strategy as needed to maximize opportunities while maintaining a healthy balance in your personal and professional life.

ANALYZING MARKET KNOWLEDGE AND EXPERIENCE

Beginner Traders:

- Start with simpler, lower-risk strategies such as long-term investing or basic swing trading. These require less intensive market monitoring and are easier to learn.

- Focus on learning fundamental and technical analysis basics to build a strong foundation.

Intermediate to Advanced Traders:

- Consider more complex strategies like day trading or position trading if you have a good grasp of market dynamics and technical indicators.

- Continuously update your knowledge and stay informed about market trends and news.

CONSIDERING MARKET CONDITIONS

Bullish Markets: In an upward-trending market, strategies that follow the trend, such as position trading or long-term investing, can be effective.

Bearish Markets: In downward-trending markets, contrarian strategies or short-term trading methods like day trading might be more appropriate.

Volatile Markets: High volatility can offer opportunities for day traders and swing traders to capitalize on rapid price movements.

COMBINING STRATEGIES

Diversification:

Don't feel restricted to a single strategy. Combining multiple strategies can help diversify risk and capitalize on different market conditions.

Example: You might use long-term investing for your core portfolio while employing swing trading for additional income generation.

Adaptive Approach:

Be flexible and adapt your strategies as market conditions and personal circumstances change. Continually reassess your goals, risk tolerance, and time commitment.

Choosing the right trading strategy is essential for aligning your trading activities with your financial goals, risk tolerance, and lifestyle. As a beginner, start by assessing your personal circumstances and gradually build your skills and knowledge.

By understanding your objectives, evaluating your risk appetite, and considering your time availability, you can select a strategy that suits your needs and enhances your chances of success in the silver market. Remember, the best strategy is one that you can stick to consistently, and that fits well with your overall investment plan.

CHAPTER 19: RISK MANAGEMENT

SETTING STOP-LOSS AND TAKE-PROFIT ORDERS

Effective risk management is crucial for silver traders to protect capital, minimize losses, and maximize profitability. This chapter explores the importance of setting stop-loss and take-profit orders, strategies for determining optimal levels, and practical tips for implementing risk management techniques in silver trading.

1. IMPORTANCE OF RISK MANAGEMENT

Risk management is a fundamental aspect of successful trading and investing. It involves identifying, assessing, and prioritizing risks followed by coordinated efforts to minimize, monitor, and control the probability or impact of unfortunate events. Effective risk management ensures capital preservation, maintains emotional discipline, and optimizes the risk-reward ratio. Here's a detailed exploration of its importance:

Capital Preservation

Protecting Trading Capital:

The primary goal of risk management is to protect your trading capital from significant losses. By limiting potential losses, you ensure that you have enough capital to continue trading and take advantage of future opportunities.

Example: Setting a stop-loss order at a predefined level helps to cap losses on any single trade. If you invest $10,000 in silver and set a stop-loss at 5%, the maximum loss you would incur on that trade is $500, preserving the majority of your capital for future trades.

Minimizing Adverse Impacts:

Risk management strategies help to minimize the impact of adverse market movements and unexpected events on your portfolio performance. This includes diversifying investments, using hedging techniques, and staying informed about market conditions.

Example: Diversifying your investments across different assets, such as physical silver, silver ETFs, and silver mining stocks, can reduce the impact of a downturn in any single market on your overall portfolio.

Emotional Discipline

Reducing Emotional Decision-Making:

Establishing predefined risk parameters and adhering to risk management rules can significantly reduce emotional decision-making. This prevents panic-selling during market downturns or over-leveraging during market upswings.

Example: By setting a maximum risk per trade, say 2% of your total trading capital, you prevent making impulsive decisions that could jeopardize your overall portfolio. For instance, if your trading capital is $50,000, you would risk no more than $1,000 on any single trade.

Maintaining Trading Discipline:

Consistent risk management practices help maintain trading discipline, ensuring that you stick to your trading plan and strategies. This helps avoid impulsive actions driven by fear or greed, especially during volatile market conditions.

Example: During a market rally, it's easy to get caught up in the excitement and take on excessive risk. By adhering to your risk management rules, you ensure that you remain disciplined and do not overextend yourself.

Optimized Risk-Reward Ratio

Enhancing Profitability:

Effective risk management balances potential losses with potential gains, enhancing overall profitability. By ensuring that your potential profits exceed potential losses in each trade, you achieve a positive risk-reward ratio.

Example: If you set a stop-loss at 5% and a take-profit level at 15%, your risk-reward ratio is 1:3. This means that for every dollar you risk, you stand to gain three dollars, optimizing your chances of overall profitability even if not all trades are successful.

Achieving Positive Risk-Reward Ratio:

Ensuring that each trade has a favorable risk-reward ratio is critical for long-term success. This involves calculating potential gains and losses before entering a trade and setting appropriate stop-loss and take-profit levels.

Example: Before entering a trade, you might identify that the potential upside of a silver investment is $1,500, while the potential downside is $500. By entering trades with such favorable ratios, you can achieve consistent gains over time.

2. SETTING STOP-LOSS ORDERS

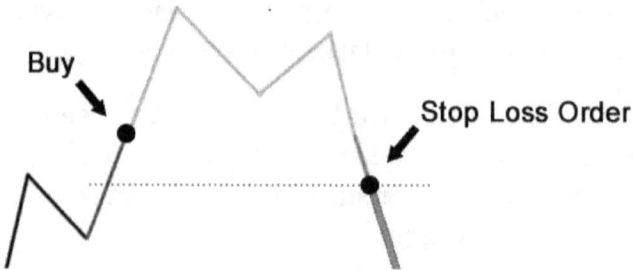

Stop Loss Order: pennystocks.com

Stop-Loss Order: An order placed with a broker to automatically sell a silver position if the price reaches a specified level.

Protects against excessive losses by limiting downside risk and preserving capital in volatile market conditions.

Strategies for Determining Stop-Loss Levels:

Technical Analysis: Identify support levels, moving averages, and key chart patterns (e.g., trendlines, Fibonacci retracements) as potential stop-loss points.

Volatility-Based Stops: Adjust stop-loss levels based on market volatility using average true range (ATR) or volatility indicators.

Risk Percentage: Set stop-loss levels based on a predetermined percentage of account equity or position size to align with risk tolerance.

Adjusting Stop-Loss Orders:

Regularly review and adjust stop-loss levels as market conditions evolve, price targets are reached, or new technical signals emerge.

Use trailing stops to lock in profits and adjust stop levels in the direction of favorable price movements to mitigate risk.

3. SETTING TAKE-PROFIT ORDERS

Take-Profit Order: An order placed to automatically close a silver position when a specified profit target is reached.

Locks in profits and ensures that traders capitalize on favorable price movements while avoiding potential reversals.

Strategies for Determining Take-Profit Levels:

Technical Analysis: Identify resistance levels, Fibonacci extensions, or previous price highs as potential take-profit targets.

Risk-Reward Ratio: Set take-profit levels to achieve a favorable risk-reward ratio, ensuring that potential gains exceed potential losses.

Trailing Take-Profit: Adjust take-profit levels dynamically to capture additional gains as price continues to move in the desired direction.

Managing Take-Profit Orders:

Monitor market conditions and adjust take-profit levels based on new developments, market sentiment shifts, or updated technical analysis signals.

Consider partial profit-taking strategies to secure initial profits while allowing remaining positions to potentially benefit from further price appreciation.

4. PRACTICAL TIPS FOR RISK MANAGEMENT

Implementing effective risk management strategies is crucial for maintaining a sustainable trading practice and achieving long-term success. Here are some practical tips to help you manage risk effectively:

Position Sizing

Determine Appropriate Position Sizes:

Assess Account Equity: Calculate the total equity in your trading account and decide on a fixed percentage of your capital to risk on each trade. This helps in controlling the potential impact of any single loss on your overall portfolio.

Example: If you have a trading account with $20,000 and you decide to risk 2% per trade, you would risk $400 per trade.

Evaluate Risk Tolerance: Understand your risk tolerance level and adjust position sizes accordingly. Conservative traders might risk less per trade, while more aggressive traders might be comfortable with higher risk levels.

Example: A conservative trader with a $20,000 account might risk only 1% per trade ($200), while an aggressive trader might risk 3% per trade ($600).

Set Stop-Loss Levels: Use stop-loss orders to define the maximum loss you are willing to accept on a trade. Position sizes should be adjusted so that the dollar amount risked per trade does not exceed your predetermined risk tolerance.

Example: If your stop-loss is set at 5% of the trade value and you are risking $400 per trade, your position size should be $8,000 (since $400 is 5% of $8,000).

Avoid Over-Leveraging:

Over-leveraging can lead to significant losses, especially during volatile market conditions. Use leverage cautiously and ensure that leveraged positions align with your risk tolerance and overall trading strategy.

Example: If you are trading on a platform that offers 10:1 leverage, a $1,000 investment controls $10,000 worth of silver. While this amplifies potential profits, it also magnifies potential losses. Ensure that leveraged trades do not exceed your risk parameters.

Allocate Capital Conservatively: Spread your capital across multiple positions and avoid concentrating too much capital in a single trade. Diversification helps to reduce the impact of adverse market movements on your overall portfolio.

Example: Instead of investing the entire $20,000 account in one trade, you might split it into five $4,000 trades, each with its own stop-loss and risk parameters.

Contingency Planning

Prepare for Unexpected Market Events:

Market events, such as unexpected economic data releases, geopolitical developments, or natural disasters, can significantly impact silver prices. Having a contingency plan helps you to react swiftly and minimize potential losses.

Example: If a geopolitical crisis suddenly spikes market volatility, having predefined rules for reducing or closing positions can help mitigate losses.

Develop Exit Strategies: Predefine exit strategies for various scenarios, including both profit targets and loss limits. This ensures that you have a clear plan for different market conditions.

Example: If silver prices reach a certain profit target, such as a 10% increase, you might decide to sell a portion of your holdings to lock in gains. Conversely, if prices drop by 5%, you might cut losses by selling off part of your position.

Stay Informed and Adaptable:

Keep abreast of market news, economic reports, and geopolitical developments that could affect silver prices. Staying informed allows you to anticipate market movements and adjust your risk management strategies accordingly.

Example: Regularly follow financial news outlets, subscribe to market analysis reports, and participate in relevant forums and discussions to stay updated.

Adjust Risk Management Strategies: Be prepared to revise your risk management strategies based on changing market conditions. Flexibility is key to effectively managing risk in a dynamic trading environment.

Example: During periods of high market volatility, you might reduce your position sizes or tighten your stop-loss levels to protect your capital.

Setting effective stop-loss and take-profit orders is essential for managing risk and optimizing profitability in silver trading. By implementing disciplined risk management practices, traders can protect capital, minimize losses, and enhance trading outcomes in the dynamic and volatile silver market. In the final chapter, we will discuss practical tips for trade execution, continuous improvement, and achieving long-term success as a silver trader.

CHAPTER 20: CREATING A TRADING PLAN

A well-defined trading plan is essential for silver traders to establish clear objectives, strategies, and guidelines for executing trades effectively. This chapter explores the importance of creating a trading plan, key components to include, and practical steps for developing a structured approach to trading silver.

1. IMPORTANCE OF A TRADING PLAN

A trading plan is a comprehensive, structured outline that guides your trading activities. It includes your trading goals, strategies, risk management techniques, and performance evaluation criteria. For beginners, a trading plan is like a roadmap that helps you navigate the complexities of the market, making your trading decisions more systematic and less influenced by emotions. Here's why having a trading plan is crucial:

A. Clarity and Direction:

Define clear trading goals, objectives, and desired outcomes to guide decision-making and strategy implementation. Maintain focus and discipline in executing trades based on predefined rules and criteria.

Short-Term Goals: Specify what you aim to achieve in the short term, such as daily or weekly profit targets.

Long-Term Goals: Set broader objectives like annual return targets or long-term wealth accumulation.

Objective Setting: Clearly outline what you want to achieve from trading, whether it's capital growth, income generation, or wealth preservation.

Strategy Implementation: Use your plan to implement trading strategies based on predefined rules and criteria. For instance, if your goal is to make a 10% return in a year, your plan should detail the strategies to achieve this.

Avoid Emotional Trading: By following a structured plan, you reduce the chances of making impulsive decisions based on emotions like fear or greed.

Consistency: Stick to your trading strategies and rules even when the market is volatile, ensuring consistent execution of trades.

B. Risk Management:

Incorporate risk management strategies, including setting stop-loss and take-profit levels, to protect capital and minimize losses. Ensure consistency in risk tolerance and position sizing across different trading scenarios.

Stop-Loss Orders: Set stop-loss levels to automatically sell a position if it reaches a certain price, minimizing potential losses.

Take-Profit Levels: Establish take-profit points to lock in gains once a trade reaches a certain profit level.

Risk Tolerance: Define your risk tolerance level, indicating how much of your capital you are willing to risk on each trade.

Position Sizing: Determine the size of your trades based on your risk tolerance. For example, if you have a high risk tolerance, you might allocate more capital per trade, whereas with a lower risk tolerance, you would trade smaller amounts.

Uniform Risk Management: Apply the same risk management principles across all trades to maintain consistency. This includes setting uniform stop-loss and take-profit levels relative to the size of each trade.

Diversification: Spread your investments across different assets to reduce risk. For example, instead of putting all your money into one type of trade, diversify across different sectors or trading instruments.

C. Performance Evaluation:

Performance evaluation is a crucial component of a successful trading plan. It allows traders to measure their progress, identify strengths and weaknesses, and make necessary adjustments to improve their trading strategies. Here's how to effectively evaluate your trading performance:

Establish Benchmarks and Metrics

Set Clear Benchmarks:

Profit Targets: Define specific profit targets for different time frames (e.g., daily, weekly, monthly). For example, aim for a 5% monthly return on your investment.

Risk Metrics: Establish acceptable levels of risk, such as a maximum drawdown percentage. This could be, for instance, a 10% loss limit on your total trading capital.

Performance Metrics:

Win-Loss Ratio: Calculate the ratio of profitable trades to losing trades. A win-loss ratio of 2:1 means you win two trades for every one you lose.

Average Profit and Loss: Track the average profit per winning trade and average loss per losing trade to ensure your profits outweigh your losses.

Risk-Reward Ratio: Assess the potential reward for each unit of risk. A risk-reward ratio of 1:3 means you risk $1 to make $3.

Sharpe Ratio: Measure the risk-adjusted return of your trades. The Sharpe ratio helps determine if the returns are due to smart decisions or excessive risk.

Maximum Drawdown: Monitor the largest peak-to-trough decline in your portfolio. This helps in understanding the risk and potential recovery time from significant losses.

Track Progress Towards Goals

Trading Journal:

Record Details: Keep a detailed record of every trade, including entry and exit points, position sizes, reasons for the trade, and outcomes.

Emotional State: Note your emotional state during each trade to understand how emotions affect your decisions.

Regular Reviews:

Monthly and Quarterly Reviews: Conduct regular reviews of your trading activities. Compare your actual performance against your benchmarks.

Trend Analysis: Identify trends and patterns in your trades. For example, determine if certain times of the day or specific market conditions yield better results.

Identify Areas for Improvement

Data-Driven Insights:

Analyze Trade Outcomes: Examine both winning and losing trades to understand what contributed to the success or failure. Identify any common factors or mistakes.

Performance Metrics Review: Regularly review your key performance metrics. If your win-loss ratio is declining, investigate the underlying reasons.

Adjust Strategies:

Refine Entry and Exit Criteria: Based on your analysis, adjust your entry and exit criteria to improve the effectiveness of your trades. For instance, if you notice that trades performed better with certain technical indicators, incorporate those into your strategy.

Risk Management Adjustments: Modify your risk management strategies based on performance reviews. If your maximum drawdown exceeds acceptable levels, tighten your stop-loss orders or reduce position sizes.

Feedback Loop:

Continuous Learning: Treat each trade as a learning opportunity. Use the insights gained from performance evaluation to continuously refine your trading plan.

Market Feedback: Stay updated with market trends and news to adapt your strategies accordingly. If new market conditions emerge, adjust your trading plan to stay relevant.

2. COMPONENTS OF A TRADING PLAN

Trading Goals and Objectives:

Define specific, measurable, achievable, relevant, and time-bound (SMART) goals for trading silver.

Set short-term and long-term objectives aligned with

financial targets, risk tolerance, and trading style.

Market Analysis:

Conduct comprehensive analysis of the silver market, including fundamental factors (supply-demand dynamics, economic indicators) and technical factors (chart patterns, indicators).

Stay informed about market news, geopolitical developments, and sector-specific trends influencing silver prices.

Trading Strategy:

Select a trading strategy (e.g., day trading, swing trading, long-term investing) based on personal preferences, risk tolerance, and market conditions.

Outline specific entry and exit criteria, technical indicators, and risk management rules for implementing the chosen strategy.

Risk Management Plan:

Define risk management parameters, including maximum risk per trade, position sizing rules, and contingency plans for adverse market scenarios.

Incorporate stop-loss and take-profit orders to manage risk and protect trading capital from significant losses.

Trade Execution:

Outline procedures for trade execution, including order placement, timing considerations, and monitoring trade progress.

Specify criteria for adjusting stop-loss levels, taking partial profits, or scaling into positions based on market conditions.

Psychological Preparation:

Address psychological factors impacting trading performance, such as maintaining emotional discipline, controlling biases, and handling stress.

Develop coping strategies for managing psychological challenges and maintaining focus during volatile market conditions.

3. PRACTICAL STEPS TO DEVELOP A TRADING PLAN

Assess Personal Preferences and Goals:

Evaluate individual trading objectives, risk appetite, time commitment, and financial resources available for trading silver.

Align trading goals with personal strengths, experience level, and commitment to continuous learning and improvement.

Research and Analysis:

Conduct thorough research on silver market fundamentals, technical analysis techniques, and trading strategies suitable for current market conditions.

Utilize reliable sources of information, educational resources, and mentorship to enhance trading knowledge and decision-making skills.

Document and Review:

Document the trading plan in a written format outlining each component, strategy, and rule for clarity and reference.

Regularly review and update the trading plan to reflect evolving market dynamics, lessons learned from previous trades, and adjustments in trading strategies.

Creating a trading plan is essential for silver traders to establish a structured approach, mitigate risks, and enhance trading effectiveness. By defining clear goals, implementing sound strategies, and integrating robust risk management techniques, traders can navigate the complexities of the silver market with confidence and achieve long-term success. In the final chapter, we will discuss essential tips for trade execution, continuous improvement, and maintaining resilience in the face of market challenges.

PART 7: EXECUTING TRADES

CHAPTER 21: PLACING BUY AND SELL ORDERS

Executing buy and sell orders effectively is crucial for silver traders to capitalize on market opportunities and implement their trading strategies. This chapter explores the process of placing buy and sell orders, considerations for order types, order execution strategies, and practical tips to optimize trade execution in the dynamic silver market.

1. UNDERSTANDING ORDER TYPES

Market Orders:

Market orders are executed immediately at the best available market price.

Purpose: Used to enter or exit positions quickly, especially in fast-moving markets or when precise execution price is less critical.

Limit Orders:

Limit orders specify a price at which the trader is willing to buy or sell.

Purpose: Control entry and exit prices to achieve specific price targets or manage slippage during volatile market conditions.

Stop Orders:

Stop-Loss Orders: Automatically trigger a market sell order when the price reaches a specified level below the current market price.

Stop-Buy Orders: Trigger a market buy order when the price reaches a specified level above the current market price, often used for breakout strategies.

Trailing Stop Orders:

Trailing Stop-Loss: Adjusts the stop-loss price dynamically as the market price moves in the trader's favor, maintaining a specified distance (e.g., percentage or dollar amount) below the market price.

Purpose: Protect profits by securing gains while allowing potential for further price appreciation.

2. CONSIDERATIONS FOR ORDER PLACEMENT

Placing orders effectively is essential to successful trading, ensuring that you enter and exit positions at optimal times and prices. Here are key considerations for order placement:

Price Levels and Execution Timing

Evaluating Market Conditions:

Current Trends: Analyze ongoing price trends using technical indicators such as moving averages, trend lines, and momentum oscillators. For instance, if silver is in an uptrend, look for pullbacks to enter long positions.

Market Sentiment: Assess market sentiment through news analysis, sentiment indices, and social media trends to gauge the general mood of investors. A positive sentiment might suggest a continuation of the current trend.

Determining Entry and Exit Points:

Support and Resistance Levels: Identify key support and resistance levels where the price has historically reversed or paused. Place buy orders near support levels and sell orders near resistance levels.

Technical Indicators: Use indicators like the Relative Strength

Index (RSI) to determine overbought or oversold conditions, signaling potential entry or exit points.

Volatility Assessment: Consider the market's volatility. In a highly volatile market, widen your stop-loss levels to avoid being stopped out by short-term price swings.

Adjusting Order Parameters:

Limit Orders: Set limit orders to buy or sell at a specific price, ensuring you enter or exit trades at your desired levels. For example, place a limit buy order slightly above a support level to increase the chances of execution.

Stop Orders: Utilize stop-loss and stop-limit orders to protect against significant losses. A stop-loss order might be placed just below a support level to minimize potential losses.

Time-in-Force (TIF) Options: Choose appropriate TIF options (e.g., Good Till Cancelled, Immediate or Cancel) based on your trading strategy and market conditions.

Order Size and Position Sizing

Calculating Position Size:

Account Equity: Base your position size on your total account equity. For instance, risk no more than 2% of your account on a single trade.

Risk Tolerance: Adjust position size according to your risk tolerance. If you are conservative, you might risk only 1% per trade.

Percentage Allocation: Determine what percentage of your trading capital you are willing to allocate to each trade. This helps in diversifying risk and avoiding overexposure.

Avoiding Over-Trading:

Trade Frequency: Set limits on the number of trades per day or week to avoid the pitfalls of over-trading, which can lead to excessive transaction costs and emotional fatigue.

Quality over Quantity: Focus on high-probability trade setups rather than placing numerous low-quality trades.

Managing Trading Capital:

Position Adjustments: Regularly review and adjust your positions based on market movements and changes in your account equity. For instance, if your account equity grows, you might increase your position size proportionately.

Market Liquidity

Choosing Liquid Instruments:

Silver Instruments: Trade silver ETFs, futures contracts, or highly liquid silver stocks to ensure sufficient market liquidity.

Volume Indicators: Use volume indicators to confirm liquidity. High trading volumes generally indicate better liquidity.

Monitoring Bid-Ask Spreads:

Spread Analysis: Keep an eye on bid-ask spreads. Narrow spreads indicate higher liquidity and lower transaction costs.

Slippage Management: In highly liquid markets, slippage is less likely. However, in low-liquidity scenarios, place limit orders to control execution prices.

Assessing Market Depth:

Order Book Analysis: Examine the order book to understand the market depth. A deeper order book with substantial buy and sell orders at various price levels indicates robust liquidity.

Adapting Strategies: If liquidity is low, adjust your trading strategy to use smaller order sizes or avoid placing large orders that might impact the market price.

3. ORDER EXECUTION STRATEGIES

Trade Confirmation:

Review order details, including quantity, order type, price, and expiration, to ensure accuracy before submission.

Verify account balances, margin requirements, and available buying power to support the planned trade.

Execution Timing:

Consider timing factors, such as market opening hours,

economic data releases, and news events that may impact silver prices.

Implement day trading or swing trading strategies based on intraday market movements and optimal trade execution windows.

Monitoring and Adjustments:

Monitor trade progress, market reactions, and technical signals to determine whether adjustments to stop-loss or take-profit levels are necessary.

Stay informed about market developments and adjust trading plans accordingly to capitalize on emerging opportunities or mitigate risks.

Placing buy and sell orders effectively is essential for silver traders to implement their trading strategies, manage risk, and optimize trade execution outcomes. By understanding different order types, considering market conditions, and utilizing effective execution strategies, traders can navigate the complexities of the silver market with confidence and achieve their financial objectives

CHAPTER 22: TIMING YOUR TRADES

Timing your trades effectively is crucial for silver traders to capitalize on market opportunities, optimize entry and exit points, and achieve trading objectives. This chapter explores the importance of timing in silver trading, factors influencing trade timing decisions, and practical strategies for identifying favorable trade windows in the dynamic silver market.

1. IMPORTANCE OF TRADE TIMING

MARKET EFFICIENCY

Identifying Optimal Entry and Exit Points:

Technical Analysis: Use technical indicators such as moving averages, Bollinger Bands, and RSI to pinpoint the best times to enter or exit trades. For example, entering a trade when the price crosses above a moving average can signal an upward trend.

Support and Resistance Levels: Place buy orders near support levels and sell orders near resistance levels to maximize gains and minimize losses.

Candlestick Patterns: Recognize candlestick patterns like Doji, Hammer, or Engulfing patterns to make informed timing decisions.

Capitalizing on Short-Term Price Movements:

Intraday Volatility: Monitor intraday price charts and utilize strategies like scalping to profit from short-term fluctuations.

High-Volume Trading Periods: Trade during high-volume periods, such as market open and close, to benefit from higher liquidity and more precise order execution.

RISK MANAGEMENT

Minimizing Exposure to Market Fluctuations:

Strategic Entry Times: Enter trades during times of lower volatility to reduce the risk of adverse price movements.

Avoiding Major News Releases: Be cautious around major economic announcements or geopolitical events that can cause significant price swings.

Implementing Stop-Loss and Take-Profit Orders:

Predefined Risk Parameters: Set stop-loss orders at strategic levels to limit potential losses. For example, placing a stop-loss just below a recent support level can protect against large downward movements.

Take-Profit Levels: Establish take-profit orders to secure gains at predefined price levels. This can be particularly effective in volatile markets where prices can quickly reverse.

OPPORTUNITY RECOGNITION

Recognizing Market Inefficiencies and Price Anomalies:

Arbitrage Opportunities: Identify and exploit discrepancies in silver prices across different markets or trading platforms.

Trend Reversals: Use indicators such as MACD or Stochastic Oscillators to spot potential trend reversals and time entries or exits accordingly.

Aligning Trade Timing with Market Events:

Fundamental News Releases: Pay attention to economic indicators like GDP growth, inflation reports, and employment data that can impact silver prices. For instance, a lower-than-expected inflation report can lead to lower demand for silver as a hedge, impacting its price.

Geopolitical Events: Monitor geopolitical developments such as trade negotiations, political instability, and central bank policies. These events can create significant trading opportunities or risks.

2. FACTORS INFLUENCING TRADE TIMING

Technical Analysis Signals:

- Utilize chart patterns, trendlines, and technical indicators (e.g., moving averages, RSI) to identify entry and exit signals.
- Confirm trade setups based on price action, volume analysis, and trend confirmation for higher probability trades.

Market Sentiment and Psychology:

- Assess investor sentiment, market psychology, and sentiment indicators (e.g., fear/greed index, COT reports) influencing silver price movements.
- Capitalize on sentiment extremes and behavioral biases to anticipate trend reversals or continuation patterns.

Economic Calendar Events:

- Monitor scheduled economic data releases (e.g., GDP reports, inflation data) and central bank announcements impacting silver and precious metals markets.
- Adjust trade timing around high-impact news events to manage volatility and potential market reactions.

3. PRACTICAL STRATEGIES FOR TRADE TIMING

INTRADAY TRADING STRATEGIES

Breakout Trading:

Identifying Breakouts: Look for price action breaking above resistance or below support levels on high volume. For instance, if silver has been trading in a range between $25 and $30, a breakout above $30 with increased volume could signal the start of a new uptrend.

Confirmation Indicators: Use momentum indicators like the RSI or MACD to confirm the strength of the breakout. A breakout accompanied by a bullish RSI crossing above 70 or a MACD crossover can provide additional confidence in the trade.

Trade Execution: Enter positions as the breakout occurs, setting stop-loss orders just below the resistance level for long trades or above the support level for short trades to manage risk.

Pullback Trading:

Trend Analysis: Identify strong trends using moving averages or trend lines. In an uptrend, look for pullbacks to key support levels, such as a 50-day moving average.

Entry Points: Enter trades during pullbacks to these support levels, anticipating a continuation of the trend. For example, if silver is in a strong uptrend and retraces to its 50-day moving average, this could be an ideal buying opportunity.

Risk Management: Place stop-loss orders below the recent low of the pullback to protect against deeper corrections.

Swing Trading Techniques

Trend Following:

Longer-Term Charts: Use daily or weekly charts to identify the direction of the prevailing trend. Trends can be identified by a series of higher highs and higher lows in an uptrend or lower highs and lower lows in a downtrend.

Technical Indicators: Rely on indicators like moving averages (e.g., 200-day MA) or the ADX to confirm trend strength. Enter trades in the direction of the trend and use trailing stop-loss orders to lock in profits as the trend progresses.

Example: If silver prices have been consistently rising and the 50-day MA is above the 200-day MA, consider entering long positions in line with the trend.

Counter-Trend Trading:

Divergence Signals: Look for divergence between price and indicators like RSI or MACD. For instance, if silver prices are making new highs but RSI is making lower highs, this could signal a potential reversal.

Candlestick Patterns: Identify reversal patterns such as Doji, Hammer, or Engulfing patterns at key support or resistance levels.

Entry and Exit: Enter trades when reversal signals are confirmed by price action, setting tight stop-loss orders to manage risk.

LONG-TERM POSITIONING

Fundamental Analysis:

Macroeconomic Trends: Align trade timing with broader economic indicators such as interest rates, inflation, and industrial demand for silver. For example, an expectation of rising inflation might prompt long-term investments in silver as a hedge.

Market Fundamentals: Consider factors such as mining production, geopolitical stability, and technological advancements that influence silver demand and supply.

4. IMPLEMENTING TRADE TIMING STRATEGIES

Pre-Trade Preparation:

- Conduct thorough market analysis and research to identify potential trade opportunities and formulate a trading plan.
- Define entry criteria, exit points, and risk management parameters to guide trade execution and decision-making.

Real-Time Monitoring:

- Stay vigilant during active trading hours, monitoring price movements, market depth, and order flow to execute trades promptly.
- Adjust trade timing based on emerging market conditions, technical signals, and news developments impacting silver prices.

Post-Trade Evaluation:
- Review trade outcomes, performance metrics, and adherence to trading plan guidelines to assess the effectiveness of trade timing strategies.
- Identify lessons learned, areas for improvement, and adjustments needed for future trades to refine trade timing skills and enhance trading success.

Effective trade timing is essential for silver traders to optimize entry and exit points, manage risk, and capitalize on market opportunities. By incorporating technical analysis signals, market sentiment indicators, and economic calendar events into trade timing strategies, traders can navigate the complexities of the silver market with confidence and achieve their trading goals. In the final chapter, we will summarize key insights, reinforce best practices for trade timing, and provide additional resources for continuous learning and improvement in silver trading.

PART 8: TOOLS AND RESOURCES FOR SILVER TRADERS

CHAPTER 23: TRADING PLATFORMS AND SOFTWARE

Choosing the right trading platform and utilizing appropriate software tools are essential for silver traders to execute trades efficiently, access market data, and analyze price movements effectively. This chapter explores the importance of trading platforms, key features to consider when selecting a platform, popular trading software tools for silver trading, and practical tips for optimizing your trading experience.

1. IMPORTANCE OF TRADING PLATFORMS

Execution Speed and Reliability: Facilitating fast order execution and minimal latency is essential to capitalize on market opportunities, especially in volatile silver markets. Ensuring platform stability and uptime helps avoid disruptions during critical trading periods, allowing traders to act swiftly and confidently.

Market Access and Instruments: Trading platforms should provide access to a wide range of silver instruments, including spot contracts, futures, options, and exchange-traded funds (ETFs). They should also support multiple asset classes and global markets to diversify trading opportunities and manage portfolio risk.

Charting and Technical Analysis Tools: Platforms must offer advanced charting capabilities, technical indicators, and drawing tools for analyzing silver price trends, patterns, and market signals. The ability to customize charts and layouts is important to suit individual trading preferences and strategy requirements.

2. KEY FEATURES OF TRADING PLATFORMS

User Interface and Navigation: An intuitive interface design with user-friendly navigation is crucial for seamless order placement, account management, and market research. Customizable dashboard and layout options allow traders to prioritize essential information and streamline their trading workflows.

Order Types and Execution Options: The platform should support various order types, such as market, limit, stop-loss, and trailing stop, to accommodate different trading strategies and risk management preferences. Direct market access (DMA) and smart routing capabilities are also important for efficient order execution and price improvement.

Real-Time Market Data and News Feeds: Access to real-time streaming quotes, market depth, and news updates is vital to stay informed about silver price movements and market developments. Integration with financial news sources, economic calendars, and analyst reports provides comprehensive market analysis. Websites like Bloomberg Markets (https://www.bloomberg.com/markets) and Reuters Finance (https://www.reuters.com/finance) are excellent sources for real-time data and news.

3. POPULAR TRADING SOFTWARE TOOLS

MetaTrader (MT4/MT5): MetaTrader platforms, available at MetaTrader (https://www.metatrader4.com), are widely used for their robust charting tools, technical indicators, and automated trading capabilities through Expert Advisors (EAs). They support algorithmic trading strategies and backtesting functionalities to optimize trading systems.

TradingView: TradingView (https://www.tradingview.com) is a web-based platform with interactive charts, social trading features, and a vast community of traders sharing insights and technical analysis. Customizable chart layouts, alert notifications, and integration with brokerage accounts facilitate seamless trade execution.

Thinkorswim (by TD Ameritrade): Thinkorswim (https://www.tdameritrade.com/tools-and-platforms/thinkorswim) is an advanced trading platform offering sophisticated charting tools, customizable screeners, and access to in-depth market research and analysis. Paper trading simulation, educational resources, and support for complex options trading strategies are also available.

Trading platforms and software tools play a pivotal role in facilitating efficient trade execution, market analysis, and decision-making for silver traders. By selecting a reliable platform with essential features, utilizing advanced trading software tools, and implementing best practices for platform usage, traders can optimize their trading experience, capitalize on market opportunities, and achieve their financial goals.

CHAPTER 24: USEFUL WEBSITES AND NEWS SOURCES

Accessing reliable information and staying updated with current events are critical for silver traders to make informed decisions and navigate market dynamics effectively. This chapter explores essential websites, news sources, and online resources that provide valuable insights, market analysis, economic data, and news relevant to silver trading.

FINANCIAL NEWS AND ANALYSIS WEBSITES

Bloomberg Markets (https://www.bloomberg.com/markets) provides real-time financial news, market analysis, and in-depth coverage of global economic developments impacting silver prices. The site offers insights from industry experts, market strategists, and economists on market trends, commodities, and precious metals.

Reuters Finance (https://www.reuters.com/finance) delivers comprehensive coverage of financial markets, commodities, and precious metals news, including silver price updates and market commentary. It features live market data, charts, and economic indicators to support informed trading decisions.

Investing.com (https://www.investing.com) offers a dedicated section for silver prices, charts, technical analysis tools, and customizable economic calendars. It provides news updates, market sentiment analysis, and community insights for silver traders and investors.

PRECIOUS METALS AND COMMODITIES WEBSITES

Kitco (https://www.kitco.com) specializes in precious metals news, market analysis, live silver prices, and charts for tracking silver price movements. It features educational articles, interviews with industry experts, and market outlook reports for silver investors.

FXStreet (https://www.fxstreet.com) covers commodities markets, including silver, with real-time price data, technical analysis, and economic news impacting precious metals. It offers insights into silver market trends, trading strategies, and volatility analysis from analysts and contributors.

Commodity.com (https://www.commodity.com) provides educational resources, market updates, and analysis on commodities, including silver, for traders and investors. It features beginner's guides, trading strategies, and historical price charts to support decision-making in silver trading.

ECONOMIC DATA AND CENTRAL BANK WEBSITES

Federal Reserve Economic Data (FRED) (https://fred.stlouisfed.org) offers access to a wide range of U.S. economic data, including inflation rates, GDP growth, and monetary policy indicators affecting silver prices. It provides historical data charts and interactive tools for economic research and analysis.

European Central Bank (ECB) (https://www.ecb.europa.eu) publishes economic reports, monetary policy decisions, and financial stability reviews impacting silver prices in the Eurozone. It offers insights into economic forecasts, inflation targets, and currency trends influencing precious metals markets.

World Bank Data (https://data.worldbank.org) provides global economic indicators, commodity price forecasts, and development data relevant to silver trading. It offers statistical tools, research publications, and country-specific economic analyses for informed decision-making.

TRADING AND FINANCIAL EDUCATION PLATFORMS

Investopedia (https://www.investopedia.com) offers comprehensive resources, tutorials, and articles on trading strategies, technical analysis, and fundamental concepts in silver trading. It provides definitions of financial terms, market insights, and educational videos for beginner to advanced traders.

TradingView (https://www.tradingview.com) features a social network for traders to share charts, ideas, and technical analysis on silver and other financial instruments. It offers customizable charting tools, trading scripts, and access to community-generated market insights.

Morningstar (https://www.morningstar.com) provides investment research, analysis, and performance data for silver ETFs, mining stocks, and related investment vehicles. It offers portfolio management tools, fund ratings, and market commentary from financial analysts and industry experts.

Accessing useful websites and news sources is essential for silver traders to stay informed, conduct thorough market analysis, and make educated trading decisions. By utilizing reliable financial news platforms, commodities websites, economic data sources, and educational resources, traders can enhance their understanding of silver market dynamics, identify profitable opportunities, and manage risks effectively.

CHAPTER 25: ALGORITHMIC AND AUTOMATED TRADING

Algorithmic and automated trading have revolutionized the silver markets by leveraging technology to execute trades efficiently, analyze market data, and manage portfolios. These advanced trading methods are sophisticated, requiring a solid understanding of both market dynamics and technical programming. They are best suited for traders who have substantial experience and resources to invest in the development and maintenance of these systems.

Beginners should gain experience with more traditional trading methods before transitioning to algorithmic strategies. This chapter aims to create awareness of algorithmic trading and prepare traders for future adoption. We will explore the principles of algorithmic trading, its benefits, implementation strategies, and considerations for experienced silver traders looking to integrate automation into their trading practices.

UNDERSTANDING ALGORITHMIC TRADING

Algorithmic trading uses computer algorithms to automatically execute predefined trading strategies based on market conditions, price movements, and quantitative analysis. These algorithms are designed to process large volumes of data, identify patterns, and execute trades with speed and precision.

Key components of algorithmic trading include quantitative

analysis, which utilizes statistical models, technical indicators, and historical data to develop trading algorithms and strategies. Execution algorithms are implemented for order execution, risk management, and portfolio optimization in real-time trading environments.

BENEFITS OF ALGORITHMIC TRADING

Algorithmic trading offers numerous benefits, including speed and efficiency. By executing trades at optimal prices and minimizing latency through automated order routing and execution algorithms, traders can react swiftly to market movements, news events, and price fluctuations, thereby seizing trading opportunities in the silver markets.

Risk management and consistency are also significant advantages. Predefined risk management rules, position sizing algorithms, and stop-loss mechanisms effectively mitigate trading risks. Furthermore, algorithmic trading ensures trading discipline and consistency in strategy execution across varying market conditions and scenarios.

IMPLEMENTATION STRATEGIES

Developing and implementing algorithmic trading strategies requires careful planning and execution. Collaboration with quantitative analysts, programmers, or algorithmic trading experts is crucial for developing customized trading algorithms tailored to the dynamics of the silver market. These algorithms must be rigorously tested using historical data, backtesting simulations, and paper trading to evaluate performance and refine strategies.

Integration with advanced trading platforms and APIs (Application Programming Interfaces) is essential for seamless execution and monitoring. Trading algorithms can be utilized for automated order placement, portfolio rebalancing, and real-time risk management in silver trading.

CONSIDERATIONS FOR ALGORITHMIC TRADING

Algorithmic trading necessitates careful consideration of market conditions and volatility. Traders must adjust algorithm parameters and trading strategies based on current market conditions, liquidity levels, and volatility in the silver markets. Continuous monitoring of algorithm performance, conducting sensitivity analysis, and implementing safeguards are vital to mitigate potential risks associated with algorithmic trading.

Regulatory compliance is another critical consideration. Adherence to regulatory guidelines, reporting requirements, and compliance standards governing algorithmic trading activities in the silver markets is mandatory. Ensuring transparency, fairness, and ethical conduct in the development, deployment, and execution of trading algorithms is essential.

FUTURE TRENDS AND INNOVATIONS

The future of algorithmic trading lies in advancements in machine learning algorithms and artificial intelligence (AI). These technologies can be leveraged for predictive analytics, pattern recognition, and adaptive trading strategies in the silver markets. AI-powered algorithms enhance decision-making capabilities, optimize trading performance, and capitalize on evolving market trends.

Algorithmic and automated trading provide silver traders with advanced tools to enhance trading efficiency, manage risks, and capitalize on market opportunities with precision and speed. By embracing algorithmic trading strategies, integrating technology-driven solutions, and adapting to regulatory frameworks, traders can optimize portfolio performance and achieve sustained success in the dynamic silver market environment.

PART 9: MANAGING YOUR EMOTIONS

CHAPTER 26: DEALING WITH TRADING STRESS AND EMOTIONS

Trading stress and emotions profoundly influence decision-making and trading performance within the silver markets. This chapter delves into the psychological aspects of trading, identifies common stressors and emotional challenges, and presents practical strategies to effectively manage emotions for enhanced trading outcomes.

UNDERSTANDING PSYCHOLOGICAL CHALLENGES IN TRADING

Trading often becomes an emotional rollercoaster characterized by highs and lows influenced by market volatility, trade outcomes, and financial stakes. Emotions such as fear, greed, impatience, and overconfidence can significantly impact trading decisions.

Additionally, traders encounter cognitive biases like confirmation bias and overreaction bias, which distort perceptions and judgment. These biases can be mitigated through awareness, self-reflection, and objective analysis of market data and trading strategies.

Furthermore, traders experience pressure from financial goals, performance expectations, and comparisons to peers or benchmarks. Setting realistic expectations, focusing on process-oriented goals, and maintaining a disciplined approach help alleviate this pressure.

STRATEGIES TO MANAGE TRADING STRESS AND EMOTIONS

Developing emotional intelligence is crucial for recognizing and regulating emotions effectively. Techniques such as mindfulness, meditation, or relaxation exercises can reduce stress levels and enhance emotional resilience during trading.

Establishing a structured trading routine with predefined times for market analysis, trade execution, and performance review fosters consistency and discipline, reducing emotional fluctuations. Robust risk management strategies, including setting stop-loss orders, managing position sizes, and diversifying portfolios, help mitigate potential losses.

Preparation of contingency plans for unexpected market events or adverse trade outcomes further reduces anxiety and enhances readiness.

COGNITIVE BEHAVIORAL TECHNIQUES FOR TRADERS

Cognitive restructuring involves identifying and challenging negative thought patterns or irrational beliefs that influence trading decisions. By replacing limiting beliefs with positive affirmations grounded in objective market analysis, traders can improve decision-making.

Visualization and mental imagery techniques help traders visualize successful trading outcomes, manage trades confidently, and navigate challenges calmly and clearly. Practicing mental imagery prepares traders to make decisions under pressure and builds psychological resilience.

Seeking support from fellow traders, mentors, or trading communities provides opportunities to share experiences, gain perspective, and receive emotional support, which are invaluable in managing trading stress.

Effectively managing trading stress and emotions is critical for silver traders to maintain focus, discipline, and mental clarity amid dynamic market conditions.

By understanding psychological challenges, implementing effective stress management strategies, and developing emotional intelligence, traders can optimize decision-making processes, minimize trading errors, and achieve consistent performance in silver trading.

CHAPTER 23: COMMON TRADING MISTAKES AND HOW TO AVOID THEM

Trading mistakes can hinder profitability and impede trading success for silver traders. This chapter identifies common pitfalls, errors, and misconceptions that traders often encounter and provides practical guidance on how to avoid these mistakes to improve trading outcomes and enhance overall performance.

1. OVERTRADING

Trading excessively, beyond your risk tolerance or trading plan, driven by impulse or emotions.

Avoidance Techniques:

Stick to Your Trading Plan: Define clear entry and exit criteria, risk-reward ratios, and position sizes based on your trading strategy.

Exercise Patience: Wait for high-probability trade setups validated by technical analysis or market indicators.

Limit Trading Frequency: Avoid chasing every market movement and prioritize quality over quantity in trades.

2. IGNORING RISK MANAGEMENT

Failing to implement proper risk management strategies, such as stop-loss orders or position sizing, leading to significant losses.

Avoidance Techniques:

Set Stop-Loss Orders: Define risk tolerance levels and implement stop-loss orders to limit potential losses on each trade.

Manage Leverage: Avoid excessive leverage and adjust position sizes based on account size and risk appetite.

Diversify: Spread risk across different assets or trades to mitigate portfolio volatility and single-trade impact.

3. EMOTIONAL TRADING

Allowing emotions (fear, revenge, greed, euphoria) to dictate trading decisions, leading to impulsive actions and irrational behavior.

Avoidance Techniques:

Develop Trading Discipline: Follow a systematic trading plan and stick to predefined entry and exit rules.

Practice Emotional Control: Recognize emotional triggers and take breaks to regain objectivity before making trading decisions.

Maintain Consistency: Avoid chasing losses or becoming overly confident during winning streaks; maintain a balanced approach to trading. Learn to cut your losses or take your wins and move on by sticking to your trading plan.

4. LACK OF TRADING STRATEGY OR PLAN

Trading without a well-defined strategy or plan, relying on intuition or unreliable sources for trade decisions.

Avoidance Techniques:

Create a Trading Plan: Define clear objectives, entry and exit criteria, risk management rules, and trading timeframes.

Backtest Strategies: Validate trading strategies using historical data to assess performance and refine trading rules.

Adaptability: Stay flexible to adjust trading strategies based on evolving market conditions and feedback from trade outcomes.

5. POOR RISK-REWARD RATIO

Entering trades with unfavorable risk-reward ratios, risking more capital than potential reward.

Avoidance Techniques:

Evaluate Risk-Reward: Assess potential trade outcomes and ensure that potential rewards justify the risk taken on each trade.

Maintain Positive Expectancy: Aim for a positive expected value (EV) by consistently selecting trades with favorable risk-reward profiles.

Adjust Position Sizing: Scale position sizes based on risk tolerance and align with risk-reward ratios to optimize profitability.

6. NEGLECTING FUNDAMENTAL AND TECHNICAL ANALYSIS

Trading without adequate market analysis, ignoring fundamental economic factors or technical indicators impacting silver prices.

Avoidance Techniques:

Conduct Comprehensive Analysis: Combine fundamental analysis (economic data, geopolitical events) and technical analysis (chart patterns, indicators) for informed trade decisions.

Stay Informed: Monitor news sources, economic calendars, and market updates to stay abreast of developments affecting silver markets.

Utilize Analytical Tools: Leverage charting tools, indicators, and market data platforms to enhance analysis accuracy and trading effectiveness.

Avoiding common trading mistakes is crucial for silver traders to maintain consistency, protect capital, and achieve long-term profitability. By recognizing potential pitfalls, implementing effective risk management strategies, and adhering to disciplined trading practices, traders can mitigate trading risks and optimize trading outcomes in the dynamic silver market.

PART 10: STAYING UPDATED AND CONTINUING EDUCATION

CHAPTER 28: KEEPING UP WITH MARKET NEWS AND TRENDS

Staying informed about market news and trends is crucial for silver traders to make informed decisions, identify trading opportunities, and navigate market volatility effectively. This chapter explores effective strategies, tools, and resources for staying updated with market news, economic trends, and geopolitical developments in silver trading.

1. IMPORTANCE OF MARKET NEWS AND TRENDS

Understanding Market Dynamics: Traders need to grasp how market news, economic indicators, and geopolitical events impact silver prices and market sentiment. Keeping abreast of macroeconomic factors, supply-demand dynamics, and industry developments is essential for informed decision-making in silver markets.

Utilizing Decision-Making Insights: Market news and trend analysis provide valuable validation for trading strategies, enabling adjustments in risk management practices and the exploitation of emerging opportunities. Traders can gain actionable insights into market sentiment, investor behavior, and regulatory changes that affect silver trading activities.

2. EFFECTIVE STRATEGIES FOR MONITORING MARKET NEWS

Utilizing News Aggregation Platforms: Accessing reputable financial news websites, news aggregators, and specialized platforms is crucial for obtaining real-time updates on silver market news and trends. Subscribing to newsletters, RSS feeds, and push notifications ensures timely alerts about significant market developments.

Leveraging Economic Calendars and Event Analysis: Economic calendars facilitate tracking of scheduled economic releases, central bank announcements, and key events that influence silver prices. Analyzing event outcomes, market reactions, and implications aids in shaping effective silver trading strategies based on economic data and policy decisions.

3. INDUSTRY REPORTS AND RESEARCH PUBLICATIONS

Accessing Research Reports: Accessing industry reports, market analysis publications, and research insights from financial institutions, brokerage firms, and industry experts provides deep insights into silver market fundamentals, price forecasts, and strategic insights essential for informed decision-making.

Engaging with Trade Associations and Forums: Participating in trade associations, industry forums, and professional networks focused on silver trading facilitates the exchange of market insights, best practices, and trading strategies. Collaboration with peers, mentors, and industry professionals helps in staying updated on market trends, regulatory changes, and industry developments.

4. CONTINUOUS LEARNING AND ADAPTATION

Utilizing Educational Resources: Enrolling in online courses, webinars, and workshops on silver trading strategies, market analysis techniques, and risk management practices ensures staying updated on evolving market trends, technological advancements, and innovative trading approaches.

Staying informed about market news and trends is essential for silver traders to enhance decision-making capabilities, capitalize on trading opportunities, and effectively mitigate risks. By leveraging effective strategies, utilizing advanced tools, and accessing reliable resources for market analysis, traders can confidently navigate silver markets, adapt to changing dynamics, and achieve long-term trading success.

CHAPTER 29: JOINING TRADING COMMUNITIES AND FORUMS

Engaging with trading communities and forums is invaluable for silver traders seeking to expand knowledge, exchange insights, and stay updated on market trends. This chapter explores the benefits of joining trading communities, strategies for active participation, and considerations for leveraging community resources in silver trading.

1. BENEFITS OF TRADING COMMUNITIES AND FORUMS

Knowledge Sharing: Trading communities provide access to expertise, trading strategies, and market insights shared by experienced traders, analysts, and industry professionals. Participants learn from diverse perspectives, trading experiences, and real-world applications in silver markets.

Networking Opportunities: Connect with like-minded traders, mentors, and peers to build professional relationships, exchange ideas, and collaborate on trading strategies. By expanding their professional network, traders can access potential career opportunities within the trading industry.

2. STRATEGIES FOR ACTIVE PARTICIPATION

Contribution and Engagement: Actively participate in discussions, pose questions, and share trading experiences to contribute valuable insights and perspectives. Offer support, guidance, and constructive feedback to fellow members to foster a collaborative and supportive trading community.

Learning and Development: Attend webinars, workshops, and educational sessions organized by trading communities to enhance trading skills, market knowledge, and technical proficiency. Seek mentorship from experienced traders, participate in trading challenges, and leverage community resources for continuous learning and development.

3. ACCESS TO MARKET INSIGHTS AND ANALYSIS

Market Updates and News: Stay informed about market trends, economic developments, and geopolitical events impacting silver prices through community-shared news updates and analysis. Discuss market forecasts, trading strategies, and potential investment opportunities based on collective insights and consensus among community members.

Technical Analysis and Tools: Exchange technical analysis techniques, charting tools, and trading indicators used for analyzing silver price movements and identifying trade setups. Collaborate on algorithmic trading strategies, backtesting methodologies, and performance optimization techniques with community members.

4. COMMUNITY GUIDELINES AND ETIQUETTE

Respect and Professionalism: Adhere to community guidelines, respect diverse opinions, and maintain professionalism in interactions with fellow traders. Avoid promotional content, spam, and misinformation to uphold community integrity and credibility.

Continuous Engagement and Contribution: Stay actively engaged in discussions, provide valuable contributions, and contribute to the growth and vibrancy of the trading community.

Share success stories, lessons learned from trading experiences, and practical tips for improving trading performance to benefit community members.

5. BUILDING LONG-TERM RELATIONSHIPS

Peer Support and Collaboration: Cultivate long-term relationships with trusted peers, mentors, and industry professionals for ongoing support, guidance, and knowledge exchange. Collaborate on research projects, joint trading initiatives, and strategic partnerships to leverage collective expertise and achieve mutual trading objectives.

Joining trading communities and forums offers silver traders a platform to enhance knowledge, network with industry peers, and stay updated on market trends essential for informed decision-making and trading success. By actively participating in communities, leveraging shared insights, and fostering professional relationships, traders can gain a competitive edge, expand their trading capabilities, and navigate dynamic silver markets with confidence.

CHAPTER 30: CONTINUOUS LEARNING AND SKILL DEVELOPMENT

Continuous learning and skill development are essential for silver traders to adapt to evolving market conditions, refine trading strategies, and achieve sustainable success. This chapter explores the importance of ongoing education, effective learning strategies, and resources for continuous skill enhancement in silver trading.

1. IMPORTANCE OF CONTINUOUS LEARNING

Adaptability to Market Changes: To succeed in silver trading, it's crucial to stay updated on market trends, regulatory updates, and economic developments that influence silver prices and market dynamics. This knowledge allows traders to adjust trading strategies and risk management techniques to seize opportunities and mitigate risks in fluctuating market environments.

Improvement of Trading Skills: Enhancing technical analysis proficiency, charting skills, and algorithmic trading capabilities through continuous learning and practice is essential. Additionally, developing a deeper understanding of market psychology, behavioral finance, and sentiment analysis empowers traders to make informed decisions.

2. EFFECTIVE LEARNING STRATEGIES

Structured Learning Plans: Create personalized learning goals, timelines, and milestones to systematically improve trading skills and knowledge in silver markets. Prioritize areas such as technical analysis, risk management, and trading psychology based on individual strengths and development needs.

Utilization of Educational Resources: Enroll in online courses, webinars, and workshops offered by reputable institutions, trading academies, and industry experts specializing in silver trading. Access educational materials like e-books and video tutorials covering diverse topics related to silver market analysis, trading strategies, and investment principles.

3. PRACTICAL SKILL ENHANCEMENT

Simulation and Practice: Utilize trading simulators, paper trading accounts, and backtesting platforms to practice trading strategies, test hypotheses, and refine execution skills. Analyze performance metrics, evaluate trade outcomes, and identify areas for improvement based on simulation results and historical data analysis.

Mentorship and Guidance: Seek mentorship from experienced traders, industry professionals, or trading coaches to gain practical insights, receive feedback, and accelerate learning curves in silver trading. Collaborate with mentors to develop personalized trading plans, set realistic goals, and navigate challenges encountered on the trading journey.

4. NETWORKING AND COLLABORATION

Industry Events and Conferences: Attend silver trading conferences, industry events, and networking sessions to engage with peers, expand professional networks, and exchange trading strategies. Participate in panel discussions, expert-led sessions, and interactive workshops to gain perspectives from market leaders and industry pioneers.

Peer Learning and Community Engagement: Join online forums, trading communities, and social media groups focused on silver trading to share insights, discuss market trends, and collaborate with fellow traders. Contribute to discussions, ask questions, and learn from diverse perspectives to broaden knowledge and enhance trading acumen.

5. COMMITMENT TO PROFESSIONAL GROWTH

Continuous Improvement Mindset: Foster a growth mindset, embrace challenges, and view setbacks as learning opportunities to strengthen trading skills and resilience in silver markets. Commit to ongoing self-assessment, reflection, and adaptation of trading strategies to align with evolving market dynamics and personal development goals.

Continuous learning and skill development are integral to achieving long-term success in silver trading. By embracing lifelong learning, leveraging educational resources, and actively participating in professional development initiatives, traders can enhance trading proficiency, capitalize on market opportunities, and sustainably grow their portfolios in silver markets.

PART 11: CONCLUSION AND NEXT STEPS

CHAPTER 31: REVIEWING WHAT YOU'VE LEARNED

Reviewing what you've learned is essential for reinforcing knowledge, identifying areas of improvement, and enhancing trading effectiveness in silver markets. This chapter focuses on the importance of self-assessment, reflection, and practical application of acquired knowledge in silver trading.

1. IMPORTANCE OF REVIEWING KNOWLEDGE

Consolidating Learning: To reinforce understanding of silver market fundamentals, trading strategies, and risk management principles, systematic review and reflection are crucial. Solidifying core concepts, technical analysis techniques, and market dynamics builds a strong foundation for informed decision-making.

Identifying Strengths and Weaknesses: Assessing individual strengths in trading skills, areas needing improvement, and performance metrics based on historical trades and market analysis helps identify knowledge gaps, behavioral patterns, and trading habits impacting trading outcomes and portfolio management.

2. STRATEGIES FOR EFFECTIVE REVIEW

Self-Assessment: Periodic self-assessment evaluates trading performance, adherence to trading plans, and achievement of predefined goals in silver trading. Reflecting on past trades, analyzing trade execution, and reviewing outcomes identify successful strategies and lessons learned from trading experiences.

Peer Feedback and Mentorship: Seeking feedback from peers, mentors, or trading communities provides external perspectives, insights, and constructive criticism on trading strategies. Collaborating with mentors to review trading decisions, refine trading approaches, and implement actionable feedback enhances trading proficiency.

3. PRACTICAL APPLICATION OF KNOWLEDGE

Real-Time Market Analysis: Applying theoretical knowledge and technical skills in real-time market analysis, trend identification, and trade execution strategies in silver markets validates trade setups and informs informed trading decisions. Utilizing charting tools, technical indicators, and fundamental analysis supports this process.

Learning from Mistakes and Successes: Embracing a growth mindset involves learning from both successful trades and trading setbacks to improve decision-making and risk management strategies. Documenting trading journal entries, analyzing trade performance metrics, and deriving actionable insights facilitate continuous improvement in silver trading.

4. CONTINUOUS IMPROVEMENT

Iterative Learning Process: Adopting an iterative learning approach by setting incremental goals, experimenting with new trading strategies, and adapting to evolving market conditions enhances trading skills. Engaging in continuous learning, staying updated on market trends, and exploring advanced trading techniques fosters sustainable growth.

Long-Term Development Goals: Defining long-term development goals, prioritizing professional growth initiatives, and committing to lifelong learning in silver trading are essential. Investing in educational resources, attending industry events, and participating in professional development opportunities expand knowledge and expertise.

Reviewing what you've learned in silver trading is crucial for reinforcing knowledge, refining trading strategies, and achieving long-term success in competitive market environments. Embracing self-assessment, seeking external feedback, and applying acquired knowledge in practical trading scenarios enhance decision-making capabilities, optimize trading performance, and capitalize on opportunities in dynamic silver markets.

CHAPTER 32: SETTING FUTURE TRADING GOALS

Setting future trading goals is crucial for silver traders to define objectives, establish a roadmap for success, and maintain focus on long-term growth and profitability. This chapter explores the importance of goal setting, strategies for defining actionable trading goals, and considerations for achieving trading aspirations in silver markets.

1. IMPORTANCE OF SETTING TRADING GOALS

Clarity and Direction: To establish direction, purpose, and motivation in silver trading endeavors, define clear and specific trading goals. Align these goals with personal aspirations, financial objectives, and professional growth ambitions to guide strategic decision-making.

Measurement and Accountability: Establish measurable benchmarks, performance metrics, and timelines to track progress, evaluate achievements, and hold oneself accountable for trading outcomes. Monitoring goal attainment, adjusting strategies as needed, and celebrating milestones help maintain momentum and sustain trading discipline.

2. STRATEGIES FOR DEFINING TRADING GOALS

SMART Goal Framework: Specific: Clearly define the desired outcome, such as achieving a targeted return on investment

(ROI) or increasing trading frequency in silver markets.

- **Measurable:** Quantify goals with specific metrics, such as percentage gains, number of successful trades, or portfolio growth targets.

- **Achievable:** Set realistic and attainable goals based on current trading skills, market knowledge, and risk tolerance levels.

- **Relevant:** Ensure goals are relevant to long-term trading objectives, aligned with market opportunities, and supportive of overall financial goals.

- **Time-bound:** Establish deadlines and timelines for goal achievement, such as monthly, quarterly, or annual targets, to create urgency and maintain focus.

Long-Term and Short-Term Goals: Differentiate between long-term goals, such as achieving consistent profitability or building a diversified silver trading portfolio, and short-term goals, such as mastering a specific trading strategy or completing a trading course. Prioritize goals based on importance, urgency, and strategic alignment with evolving market conditions and personal development objectives.

3. CONSIDERATIONS FOR ACHIEVING TRADING ASPIRATIONS

Risk Management and Capital Preservation: Integrate risk management principles, such as setting stop-loss orders, diversifying portfolio investments, and managing leverage effectively, to protect capital and mitigate trading risks. Align trading goals with risk tolerance levels, financial constraints, and market volatility to sustain long-term trading viability and minimize potential losses.

Continuous Learning and Adaptation: Commit to ongoing education, skill development, and market research to enhance trading proficiency, adaptability, and resilience in silver markets. Embrace feedback, learn from trading experiences, and adjust strategies based on market trends, technological advancements, and regulatory changes affecting silver trading activities.

4. REVIEW AND ADJUSTMENT OF GOALS

Periodic Evaluation: Conduct regular reviews of trading goals, assess progress towards goal attainment, and adjust strategies or timelines as necessary to optimize trading performance. Reflect on achievements, identify areas for improvement, and leverage lessons learned from both successful trades and trading setbacks to refine future trading goals.

Adaptability to Market Conditions: Remain flexible and adaptable in goal setting, considering shifts in market dynamics, economic factors, and geopolitical events influencing silver prices and trading opportunities. Pivot strategies, explore new trading approaches, and seize emerging market trends to capitalize on evolving silver market conditions and achieve trading aspirations.

Setting future trading goals provides silver traders with a strategic framework to define objectives, track progress, and navigate towards sustainable success in competitive market environments. By adopting a SMART goal framework, prioritizing risk management, and embracing continuous learning and adaptation, traders can enhance trading proficiency, achieve long-term profitability, and realize their full potential in silver trading.

CHAPTER 33: RESOURCES FOR FURTHER STUDY

Accessing comprehensive resources is crucial for silver traders seeking to deepen knowledge, refine trading skills, and stay updated on industry trends. This chapter explores valuable resources, including books, websites, courses, and tools, to facilitate ongoing study and continuous development in silver trading.

1. BOOKS AND PUBLICATIONS

"The Silver Manifesto by David Morgan and Christopher Marchese:

Explore insights into the historical significance, market dynamics, and investment strategies related to silver trading.

Trading Silver: How to Make Money Trading Silver Futures by Glenn Ward:

Gain practical guidance on trading strategies, technical analysis, and risk management techniques specific to silver futures markets.

Technical Analysis of the Financial Markets: A Comprehensive Guide to Trading Methods and Applications by John J. Murphy:

Learn foundational principles of technical analysis, charting techniques, and market indicators applicable to silver trading.

Financial News and Publications:

Access reputable financial news sources, such as Bloomberg, Reuters, and CNBC, for real-time updates, market analysis, and economic insights affecting silver prices.

2. ONLINE COURSES AND WEBINARS

Investopedia Academy - Technical Analysis Course:

Enroll in online courses offering in-depth training on technical analysis techniques, chart patterns, and trading strategies applicable to silver markets.

Coursera - Financial Markets and Investment Strategy Specialization:

Participate in specialization programs covering financial markets, investment strategies, and portfolio management principles relevant to silver trading.

Webinars and Workshops:

Attend webinars hosted by trading platforms, industry experts, and financial institutions to explore advanced trading strategies, market trends, and risk management practices in silver trading.

3. TRADING PLATFORMS AND TOOLS

TradingView:

Utilize advanced charting tools, technical indicators, and customizable analysis features to conduct technical analysis and monitor silver price movements.

MetaTrader 4 (MT4) and MetaTrader 5 (MT5):

Access trading platforms offering comprehensive trading functionalities, automated trading options, and real-time market data for silver trading.

Bloomberg Terminal:

Subscribe to Bloomberg Terminal for comprehensive financial data, news updates, and analytical tools essential for informed decision-making in silver markets.

4. INDUSTRY ASSOCIATIONS AND FORUMS

Silver Institute:

Join industry associations, such as the Silver Institute, to access research reports, market analysis, and industry insights on silver supply-demand dynamics and market trends.

Trading Forums and Communities:

Participate in online trading forums, social media groups, and community platforms focused on silver trading to exchange ideas, share experiences, and collaborate with fellow traders.

5. EDUCATIONAL WEBSITES AND RESOURCES

Investopedia and Seeking Alpha:

Explore educational articles, tutorials, and expert analysis on silver trading strategies, market trends, and investment opportunities.

SilverSeek.com:

Visit specialized websites like SilverSeek.com for news updates, market commentary, and investment research specific to silver markets.

Accessing diverse resources for further study empowers silver traders to expand knowledge, refine trading skills, and navigate market complexities with confidence. By leveraging books, online courses, trading platforms, industry associations, and educational websites, traders can stay informed, adopt advanced trading strategies, and achieve long-term success in silver trading.

APPENDICES

GLOSSARY OF TERMS

Understanding key terms and concepts is crucial for navigating the silver trading market effectively. This glossary provides definitions for essential terms used in silver trading, helping beginners build a strong foundation of knowledge.

A

Ask Price: The lowest price at which a seller is willing to sell a security or commodity.

Asset: Any resource with economic value owned by an individual, corporation, or country, including commodities like silver.

B

Bear Market: A market condition characterized by declining prices, often by 20% or more, indicating widespread pessimism.

Bid Price: The highest price a buyer is willing to pay for a security or commodity.

Bull Market: A market condition characterized by rising prices, indicating widespread optimism.

C

Candlestick Chart: A type of financial chart used to represent price movements, showing the opening, closing, high, and low prices for a specific period.

CFD (Contract for Difference): A financial instrument that allows traders to speculate on price movements without owning the underlying asset.

Commodity: A basic good used in commerce that is interchangeable with other goods of the same type, such as silver.

D

Day Trading: The practice of buying and selling financial instruments within the same trading day.

Diversification: A risk management strategy that mixes a wide variety of investments within a portfolio.

E

Exchange-Traded Fund (ETF): A type of security that involves a collection of securities—such as stocks—that often tracks an underlying index.

Exponential Moving Average (EMA): A type of moving average that gives more weight to recent prices to make it more responsive to new information.

F

Futures Contract: A legal agreement to buy or sell a particular commodity or asset at a predetermined price at a specified time in the future.

Fundamental Analysis: The method of evaluating a security by attempting to measure its intrinsic value, analyzing economic, financial, and other qualitative and quantitative factors.

G

Geopolitical Risk: The risk of financial loss due to political instability or changes in the political landscape in a country or region.

H

Hedging: An investment strategy used to reduce the risk of adverse price movements in an asset, often by taking an offsetting position in a related security.

I

Indicator: A statistical measure or calculation used to gauge market conditions or to predict financial or economic trends.

Intrinsic Value: The actual value of a company or an asset based on its fundamentals, as opposed to its market value.

L

Leverage: The use of borrowed funds to increase one's trading position beyond what would be available from their cash balance alone.

Limit Order: An order to buy or sell a security at a specified price or better.

M

Margin: The amount of money that an investor borrows from a broker to buy securities.

Market Order: An order to buy or sell a security immediately at the best available current price.

O

Option: A financial derivative that gives the buyer the right, but not the obligation, to buy or sell an asset at a predetermined price within a specified time period.

P

Portfolio: A collection of investments owned by an individual or an institution.

Position: The amount of a particular security or commodity held by an individual or an institution.

R

Resistance Level: A price point at which a security or commodity experiences selling pressure and typically struggles to move higher.

Risk Management: The process of identification, analysis, and acceptance or mitigation of uncertainty in investment decisions.

S

Scalping: A trading strategy that involves making numerous trades over very short periods to capture small price movements.

Spread: The difference between the bid price and the ask price of a security or commodity.

Stop-Loss Order: An order placed with a broker to buy or sell once the stock reaches a certain price, designed to limit an investor's loss on a position.

Support Level: A price point at which a security or commodity experiences buying pressure and typically does not fall below.

T

Take-Profit Order: An order placed with a broker to sell a security when it reaches a certain price, designed to lock in a profit.

Technical Analysis: The method of evaluating securities by analyzing statistics generated by market activity, such as past prices and volume.

V

Volatility: A statistical measure of the dispersion of returns for a given security or market index, often associated with the level of risk.

FREQUENTLY ASKED QUESTIONS

This FAQ section addresses common questions and concerns that beginners may have about silver trading. It provides concise and informative answers to help new traders build confidence and knowledge in the silver market.

1. What is silver trading?

Silver trading involves buying and selling silver, either in physical form (such as bullion and coins) or through financial instruments like futures, options, ETFs, and CFDs, with the aim of making a profit from price movements.

2. Why should I trade silver?

Silver is a popular trading asset due to its historical value, industrial uses, and status as a safe-haven asset. Traders are attracted to silver for its price volatility, liquidity, and the potential for hedging against inflation and economic uncertainty.

3. How do I start trading silver?

To start trading silver:

Educate yourself about the silver market and trading strategies.

Choose a reputable forex or commodity trading platform.

Open and fund a trading account.

Develop a trading plan and strategy.

Start trading in a demo account before transitioning to a live account.

4. What factors influence silver prices?

Silver prices are influenced by:

Supply and demand dynamics.

Economic indicators and industrial demand.

Inflation and currency fluctuations.

Geopolitical events and market sentiment.

Government policies and central bank actions.

5. What are the risks associated with silver trading?

Risks in silver trading include:

Market volatility and price fluctuations.

Leverage risk, leading to amplified losses.

Counterparty risk with brokers and trading platforms.

Liquidity risk, especially in times of market stress.

Regulatory and geopolitical risks affecting market stability.

6. What is the difference between spot silver and silver futures?

Spot silver refers to the current market price for immediate delivery, while **silver futures** are contracts to buy or sell silver at a predetermined price on a future date. Futures allow for hedging and speculation on price movements.

7. Can I trade silver with a small amount of capital?

Yes, you can trade silver with a small amount of capital by using leverage provided by brokers. However, leverage increases both potential profits and risks, so it's important to manage risk carefully.

8. What is leverage in silver trading?

Leverage allows traders to control a larger position with a smaller amount of capital. For example, a 10:1 leverage ratio means you can control $10,000 worth of silver with just $1,000. While leverage can magnify profits, it also increases the potential for significant losses.

9. How can I manage risk in silver trading?

Risk management strategies include:

Setting stop-loss and take-profit orders.

Diversifying your trading portfolio.

Using appropriate leverage levels.

Continuously educating yourself and staying informed about market conditions.

Regularly reviewing and adjusting your trading plan.

10. What tools and indicators are useful for silver trading?

Useful tools and indicators for silver trading include:

Technical analysis tools like moving averages, RSI, and MACD.

Fundamental analysis sources, including economic calendars and news feeds.

Charting software to analyze price patterns and trends.

Risk management tools like stop-loss and limit orders.

11. Where can I find reliable information about silver trading?

Reliable information can be found on:

Financial news websites like Bloomberg, Reuters, and CNBC.

Educational websites like Investopedia and Seeking Alpha.

Industry reports from organizations like the Silver Institute.

Trading platforms that offer research tools and market analysis.

12. How do I choose the right broker for silver trading?

When choosing a broker, consider:

Regulation and reputation.

Trading platform features and usability.

Fees and commissions.

Customer support and educational resources.

Availability of trading instruments and leverage options.

Understanding these key aspects can help you make informed decisions and navigate the silver market more confidently. Always continue learning and seeking reliable information to enhance your trading skills and success.

ABOUT THE AUTHOR

Usiere Uko

Usiere Uko is a Consultant, ILO Certified Trainer, and Business & Finance Author focused on financial independence and entrepreneurship. A former oil and gas engineer turned entrepreneur, he helps individuals and business owners build sustainable income, make smarter financial decisions, and grow resilient businesses.

He is a certified Business Development Service Provider (BDSP) and an ILO-certified trainer in SIYB and WIDB, and currently serves as Lead Consultant at Sageway Consulting and Training Coordinator at The Citadel Business Academy.

Usiere writes in a friendly and practical style, making complex financial and business ideas simple, clear, and actionable for everyday readers and entrepreneurs. He is based in Lagos, Nigeria.

BOOKS IN THIS SERIES
COMMODITIES TRADING FOR BEGINNERS

Gold Trading 101: The Beginner's Guide To Unlocking The Potential Of Precious Metals

Silver Trading 101: Smart Strategies For Silver Trading Beginners

Oil Trading 101: Understanding The Basics Of Trading The Oil Market, Cfds, Futures And Options

Natural Gas Trading 101: A Beginner's Guide To Profiting From The Energy Market

BOOKS BY THIS AUTHOR

Practical Steps To Financial Freedom And Independence: Money Management Skills For Beginners

Before You Trade Forex: Things You Need To Know If You Desire To Start Trading Forex Profitably

Before You Invest In Cryptocurrency: A Simple Guide To Understanding The Cryptocurrency Market

101 Common Money Mistakes To Avoid: And How To Fix Them. Book 1: Expenses. Money Management, Making Your Budget Work

How To Avoid Living Under Financial Pressure: A Simple Guide To Getting Back Control Of Your Finances

Financial Independence For Employees: Making

Your Job A Stepping Stone To Exiting The Rat Race And Living Your Dreams

Managing Your Money Post Covid: Financial Management Skills For An Era Of High Inflation And Market Disruption

Retire On Your Own Terms: A Simple Guide To Financially Literate Retirement Planning

Your Ultimate Money Makeover: Manage Your Money Better, Take Control Of Your Finances And Your Life

Teaching Kids Money 101: Simple Parenting Strategies For Raising Financially Literate Kids From Toddler To Teen Years And Beyond

Uncle Ben's Money Lessons: Book I: Do You Want To Work For Money? A Vacation Story With An Adventure Into The World Of Money

Nft Investing 101: A Beginner's Guide To Collectible Digital Assets

Stock Market Investing 101: A Practical Beginners

Guide To Online And Offline Stock Trading

Investing In Etfs 101: A Beginner's Guide For Building Wealth With Exchange-Traded Funds

Day Trading 101: A Complete Beginner's Guide To Trading The Markets

Forex Trading 101: A Beginner's Guide And Strategies To Profitable Currency Trading

Options Trading 101: A Beginner's Guide To Trading Stock Options

Futures Trading 101: A Step-By-Step Guide And Strategies For Beginner Traders

www.ingramcontent.com/pod-product-compliance
Lightning Source LLC
Chambersburg PA
CBHW071918210526
45479CB00002B/470